FANCY RATS

Judith Lissenberg

FANCY RATS

REBO PUBLISHERS

© 2003 Zuid Boekprodukties
© 2006 Rebo Publishers

Text and photographs: Judith Lissenberg
Cover design and layout: AdAm Studio, Prague, The Czech Republic
Typesetting and pre-press services:
A.R. Garamond, Prague, The Czech Republic
Translation: Guy Shipton for First Edition Translations, Cambridge, UK
Proofreading: Sarah Dunham, Jeffrey Rubinoff

ISBN 13: 978-90-366-1108-4
ISBN 10: 90-366-1108-3

CONTENTS

1 Making the rat's acquaintance 6
2 The rat in the past and present . . .16
3 Choosing and buying a rat 26
4 Handling rats 40
5 Rat accommodation 52
6 Eating and drinking 62
7 Health .72
8 Breeding rats 94
9 Colors and varieties 108
10 Glossary 122
11 Rats on the Internet 126
12 Credits and Photography 128

1 MAKING THE RAT'S ACQUAINTANCE

Horrific or adorable?

Can there be any other animal to engender such powerful feelings and opposing reactions in people as the rat? Some people shudder just at the thought of rats or even become panic-stricken by them. They see the rat as a dirty and aggressive animal, ready to leap out of toilet bowls without warning, and attack. Conversely, others see the rat as a cuddlesome creature, full of character, with whom you can build a special relationship. In reality, the rats responsible for gruesome bloodbaths in horror films are specially trained, extremely sociable animals that, in exchange for a tasty reward, will leap, run, gnaw, or "attack" on command. Yet despite its special qualities, the intelligent and friendly rat has been able to rise above its bad reputation only with difficulty. Some American rat enthusiasts have even entertained the idea of coming up with another name for their animals, such as Raffins or Norvies (deriving from *Rattus norvegicus*, the Latin name for the rat). However, in the end, the rat has remained the rat.

Young agouti fancy rat

The rodent family

Rats are mammals and belong to the order of rodents, or Rodentia. This word derives from the Latin word *rodere*, which means "to gnaw." More than half of all mammals belong to this gnawing group. All rodents have sets of two strikingly large incisors in both their upper and lower jaws. Rodents vary widely in size from the Eurasian harvest mouse, which weighs only around one third of an ounce (10 grams), to the South American capybara, which weighs on average 110 lbs (50 kg). Within the order of rodents, rats belong under Muridae, the family of mice and rats. Members of this family are somewhere between mice and rabbits in terms of size and are distinguished by their high fertility and adaptability. Rats and mice belong to the same subfamily. They are classified according to size: any smaller than roughly six inches (15 cm) and they are counted as mice, any larger and they belong

The largest and smallest of the small rodents: a fancy rat with a Chinese (dwarf) hamster

among the rats. Nevertheless, mice and rats are animals with different habits and requirements. As a pet, the fancy rat is the largest representative in the category of small rodents, which includes, in addition to the rat, the (dwarf) hamster, gerbil, and mouse.

The brown rat

Our fancy rats descend from the brown rat *(Rattus norvegicus)*, also sometimes referred to as the Norway rat or sewer rat. The brown rat originated in Asia and from its native habitat has managed to conquer the whole world. Brown rats live anywhere where they can find food and shelter, such as cellars, sewers, and barns. They are often to be found in the vicinity of water. The brown rat is an omnivore that, in addition to seeds, grain, and vegetable matter, also likes to eat eggs, small animals, and refuse. Brown rats can be compared with fancy rats to some degree in the same way as wolves and dogs. Although genetically the same as the brown rat and able to interbreed, the fancy rat, just like the dog, is a domesticated animal (a pet) that is no longer equipped to live in the wild.

The fancy rat's passport entry
Scientific name: Rattus norvegicus (domesticus)
Age: 1 to 4 years old (usual lifespan: 2 to 3 years)
 Weight: 7 to 21 ounces (200 to 600 grams)
Length: body 8 to 10 inches (22 to 26 cm); tail 7 to 8 inches (18 to 22 cm)

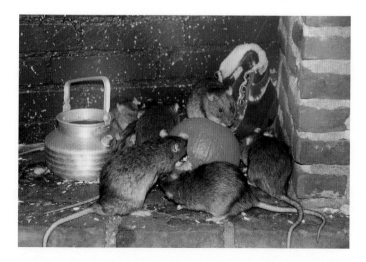

Rats are omnivores

The Black Rat

The black rat (*Rattus rattus*) is a close relative of the brown rat, and thus of the fancy rat as well. It is also referred to as "roof rat" or "ships' rat" and, just like the brown rat, originally came from Asia. The black rat is lighter, more slender, and more agile than its brown cousin. It has a more mouse-like appearance, a longer tail, and larger eyes. In contrast to the brown rat, the black rat is not so fond of water and damp cellars, and prefers dry holds in ships or attics. It eats everything but has a predilection for dry, vegetarian items, such as cere-

Rats like to live communally

al grains. Although black and brown rats are closely related, and both have 42 chromosomes, they do not interbreed. As far as is known, attempted crossings have failed to produce any living young. In the past, descendants of the black rat were also kept as pets and even bred in a number of color varieties, but these animals lost out ultimately to the domesticated descendants of the brown rat.

Not true rats

There are many rat-like animals that, while they belong among rodents, or contain the word "rat" in their name, do not belong to the fancy rat's immediate family. For example, the muskrat or musquash, sometimes also known as the water rat, is not a true rat, but belongs to the vole family. This also applies to the European and Asian water vole, which is also known as the water rat, and appeared as "Ratty" in The Wind in the Willows by Kenneth Grahame. The strapping coypu may seem like a very large rat but is more closely related to the porcupine. The slender African or Gambian giant pouched rat is a rat-like animal belonging to the genus Cricetomys. It has cheek pouches and an extremely keen sense of smell, and in Africa, has even been trained to sniff out landmines.

Real athletes

Owing to their muscularity, streamlined physique, and well-developed senses, rats are excellent at climbing, jumping, running, digging, and swimming. Rats have good ears. They can

Whiskers act as antennae

hear better and at higher pitches than humans, and recognize their owner's voice. In addition, rats have very sensitive noses that they use to search for food and to communicate and recognize their companions. Smell plays an extremely important part in a rat's activities. They often move ahead along established routes, known as "rat runs," marked along their length with traces of urine. This enables them to cover distances of up to of several miles. The sense of taste is also very important to a rat. Its whiskers are very sensitive and help it to navigate within its surroundings. Rats depend more on their ears and nose than they do on their eyes. They are short-sighted and do not see as clearly as humans, although they do see better in the dark. It seems that rats with red eyes are more sensitive to light and are not as good at perceiving depth as rats with black eyes. This explains why red-eyed rats rock their heads to and fro. This behavior is called head bobbing. They do this to get a better sense of their environment.

The rat and its "thermostatic" tail

The rat's long tail, which makes so many people squirm, is actually a smart piece of technology. It is covered in fine hair, is scaly, and is composed of dozens of circular segments. A rat's tail serves a number of important functions. For example, it plays a role in keeping the animal's balance. If you pick a rat up, it will often start swishing its tail energetically from side to side in an attempt to find some purchase. In addition, a rat is able to dissipate its excess body heat through its tail, which acts as a thermoregulator. Large blood vessels run late-

A rat's tail also acts as a rudder

rally along the length of a rat's tail, close under the surface of the skin. The blood vessels expand when the rat's body temperature rises. This enables more blood to flow to the tail, with more heat being lost through the surface of the skin. This also works the other way round: when it is cold, less blood travels to the tail in order to conserve heat.

Establishing the pecking order

Behavior

Whether wild or domestic, rats are true social animals. In nature, they live in family groups that defend their habitat against intruders. They spread their scent around their territory by urine marking or by rubbing against some object with the sides of their bodies, which contain scent glands. Family members recognize each other by their smell and strengthen the bonds between them by grooming each other's coats. In the wild, rats may live in groups (also known as troops, packs, or colonies) of ten to a hundred, or even more. They inhabit rat "burrows" that consist of a system of chambers and tunnels. Wild rats are particularly active during twilight hours, but they are not typically nocturnal animals. Domestic rats are also active during the day.

Rat language

Rats communicate with each other by means of smell, body language, and sound. When establishing his rank, a dominant rat will overturn a submissive rat and keep it pressed to the ground. Moreover, the subordinate rat will lie still on its back or side and allow itself to be sniffed at. There may also be a confrontation, with the rats standing upright like boxers, nose to nose. When this kind of conflict escalates the fur can literally fly. The body, head, ears, tail, and coat all play a role in rat language. A rat that is insecure or scared will move its ears back and forth. A curious rat collecting information about its surroundings will sit upright, point its head and ears forward, and sniff at the air. If a rat extends its body and raises a paw, it is being a little more cautious about investigating its environment. Brief grooming movements and tail swishing or wagging may point to tension. An arched back and piloerection (hair standing on end) are signs of anger and aggression. In addition to these gestures, rats possess an extensive vocabulary. They can produce very high-pitched sounds that are not always within the audible range of humans. Submissive rats often emit brief, little squeaks. Squeaks of excitement or surprise can often be heard as well during grooming sessions and romping about. Researchers have not dismissed the possibility that the cries emitted by rats playing can be equated with human laughter. A short, shrill squeak indicates annoyance; a long continuous squeak, fear. A long squeal is an expression of pain, and fighting rats may screech, hiss, and chatter their teeth.

Teeth grinding (brux)

Teeth grinding is typical rat behavior and is often compared to the purring of a cat. Rats often do this when relaxed. While grinding its teeth, the rat will sit still, frequently with eyes half-open or else bulging out slightly as a result of the jaw movements; this is known as "eye-boggle." However, teeth grinding can also be a sign of stress or insecurity.

Raising a paw

2 THE RAT IN THE PAST AND PRESENT

The advance of the rat

People and rats have been living together for centuries. The black rat *(Rattus rattus)* sought the company of humans much earlier on than the brown rat *(Rattus norvegicus)*. Historical documents indicate that the brown rat came to Europe and America only in the eighteenth century. Reports from this time describe how large numbers of rats were moving from one region to another. In one case, in 1727, hordes of rats swam across the River Volga. This occurred a few days before an earthquake, which these animals probably anticipated. However, notwithstanding the historical documentation, it is postulated that brown rats may have been present in Europe well before this. While the numbers of black rats declined, their brown relatives advanced. Brown rats were not scared of water and climbed aboard ships on mooring ropes and anchorage chains—and in so doing they conquered the world.

A bad reputation

Above all else, wild rats owe their bad reputation to a superfast reproduction rate, an unparalleled desire to gnaw on

Wild brown rats

Black rat, a print from ca. 1900

things, and the transmission of diseases. They cause a great amount of damage by eating into and contaminating food stocks. One of the diseases most commonly transmitted by wild brown rats is Leptospirosis (also known as Weil's disease in its second phase). This pathogen enters surface water through rats' urine. People can become infected if they come into contact with this water through any broken skin or any mucosal surfaces, such as the eyes and nose. In the past, it was the black rat that was responsible for causing the spread of mass disease, in particular bubonic plague, which slew millions of victims in Europe, most notably in the fourteenth century, but with epidemics occurring in the seventeenth century as well. In fact, it was not the rat itself that transmitted the plague, but the rat flea. But the keepers of fancy rats have nothing to fear as far as the transmission of terrifying diseases is concerned.

Rat kings

"Rat kings" have appeared in history every so often, a particular phenomenon in which a number of rats are found with their tails entangled and growing together. As yet, there has been no definitive scientific explanation for this. Only a few dozen rat kings have been documented, and, of these, only a few have been put on display in museums. Rat kings appear principally among black rats. The largest and most celebrated ever discovered was the (mummified) rat king of Buchheim, Germany, where, in 1828, 32 dead black rats were found with their tails knotted together.

From rat catcher to rat breeder

Rat catchers had their hands full containing the damage caused by rats' appetites and their gnawing. Ironically, it was these rat catchers who oversaw the birth of the domesticated rat. In England, at the beginning of the nineteenth century, rats were trapped and bred for the "rat pits": animal-baiting enclosures, boarded on all sides, in which dogs, usually terriers, and sackfuls of rats were let loose on one another. The dog that killed the most rats in the shortest time was proclaimed the champion. It was very popular form of entertainment, and considerable bets were placed on the outcome. Usually, a dog needed only a few seconds to kill a rat. In 1862, a dog called Jacko, owned by one Jimmy Shaw from London, established a world record by killing a thousand rats in a hundred minutes. It was the same Jimmy Shaw who collected unusually colored rats from the rat pits in order to breed from them. A fellow Londoner, Jack Black, the royal rat catcher to Queen Victoria, also did this. In the period from the 1840s through to the 1860s, he bred albino, black, fawn, gray, and piebald animals and sold them as pets. In 1898, a book appeared entitled *Full Revelations of a Professional Rat-catcher*, in which Englishman Ike Matthews wrote about his 25 years of experience in catching rats. He also discussed how to keep rats in holding cages. He believed that if you looked after the

Lazing away together

animals properly, it was perfectly possible to keep them alive for a year at least. His accommodation advice: put young rats together with young rats and old rats with old, keep them in a warm, dark place, and provide lots of water.

Hamelin

The most famous rat catcher of them all is without a doubt the one from Hamelin—the Pied Piper. The story of the Pied Piper of Hamelin is famous worldwide and has been translated into dozens of languages. In 1284, according to tradition, an extraordinary man arrived in the town of Hamelin (known today in Germany as Hamelin), and promised to deliver the local inhabitants from a plague of rats. Playing his flute, he enticed the rats to the river, where they drowned. As he was not paid for his work, he returned to Hamelin later to lure away all the town's children. The town of Hamelin still styles itself as "The Pied Piper's Town," and each year stages an open-air play about his exploits.

Miss Mary Douglas

Nowadays, rats are accepted by society as house pets, but in the past it was anything but normal to be interested in the animals. The person who was the first to become deeply involved in the promotion of rats and mice as pets, and who entered the history books as "the mother of the rat fancy," was one Mary Douglas. She was born in England in 1856, at a time when keeping rodents was considered extremely unusual, and species such as hamsters and gerbils had yet to make an appearance as house pets. The fact that Mary kept rats was particularly extraordinary because of her background. After all, she had been born into a very well-to-do, aristocratic family. Mary was, to put it mildly, quite an eccentric. She had

Rats are very athletic

a manly appearance and dressed accordingly. Sometimes, she would set off outdoors on her pony, dressed in long pants, with a large straw hat on her head and a pipe in her mouth. In 1895, the National Mouse Club was founded in England, and it drew up a breed standard for differently colored varieties of mice and held competition shows. In 1901, Mary wrote a letter to the National Mouse Club asking whether rats could also be admitted to the shows alongside mice. This is what subsequently followed, and thanks to her efforts rats enjoyed a marked growth in popularity in England. In 1912, the National Mouse Club became the National Mouse and Rat Club. Mary Douglas died in 1921 at the age of 65. After her death, the fortunes of rats took a downturn. In 1929, the National Mouse and Rat Club decided to go back to calling

While grooming

itself simply the National Mouse Club, and colored varieties were (temporarily) lost. It was only decades later that there was a resurgence of interest in rat keeping. The National Fancy Rat Society was founded in England in 1976—the very first organization established solely for rats. Afterward, rat fanciers began to organize in other countries as well, including the United States, where the first club—the Mouse and Rat Breeders Association—was set up in 1978. At first, rats seemed to be the domain of students and anti-establishment "punk rocker" types, but that soon changed. Over the past couple of decades, rats have become popular pets, appreciated in particular for their personalities, as well as being conveniently pocket-sized and relatively easy to care for.

Laboratory rats

Although rats had been used in experiments previously, they came to the fore as laboratory animals at the end of the nineteenth century. From around 1900 onward, work was done on creating special strains of albino laboratory rats, and eventually through major inbreeding and selection rats with virtually uniform characteristics could be reproduced. It was important for these animals to be virtually identical in order to carry out tests and compare their results properly. One of the most famous strains of laboratory rats was the Wistar rat, named after the Wistar Institute of Anatomy and Biology in Philadelphia, where, in 1906, Dr. Henry Donaldson began to create a pure colony of rats. The Wistar rat was the first standardized laboratory rat. It is estimated that more than half of all laboratory rats are descended from the original Wistar line. Thanks to the rat, we have gained not only a great deal of knowledge about our own health and heredity, but also about behavior. Rats are used frequently in cognitive experiments using mazes and the "Skinner box," named after American

An attractive silver fawn rat

behavioral scientist B.F. Skinner (1904–1990), who employed it to help determine certain patterns of conditioning. The Skinner box is a box with a lever and an opening that dispenses food. One of the things learned by rats in the box is that pushing on the lever can deliver food.

Temple rats

Rats are not only trapped or petted, but are also venerated. Shri Karni Mata is a Hindu temple in India, built of marble and inhabited by sacred rats. Thousands of black rats live there, fed by worshipers with milk, grain, and candies. People visit to ask for prosperity and good fortune, and drink from the same milk as the rats. Additional good fortune is bestowed on anyone who sights one of the rare white rats in the temple.

Competitions

Shows are organized in many countries where specially trained judges award points based on a rat's external appearance. During these events, you can often meet with other rat fanciers or purchase new animals. Just for fun, perhaps, you might enjoy entering your own rats into a competition. Your rat must be easy to handle in order to take part in a competition. Apart from that, the animal must not be sick or visibly gestating, and must not have wounds, injuries to, for examp-

*The head should
not be too pointed*

*The head should
not be too pointed*

le, the ears or tail, or have parasites. The rat travels to the show
in a special transportation box that is kitted out with water,
nesting material, and some food to eat during the journey. All
boxes are numbered and set out on tables in order of color and
age classes. The judge takes the animals out of their accommodation one by one to assess them against the breed standard. Each rat's strong points and weaker points are then
recorded on a scorecard. Rats with the highest scores have the
chance to become winners of the "Best Variety" or even "Best
Rat in Show," and are then awarded a (modest) prize.

Breed standard

A breed standard has been established in order to judge rats
according to their external appearance. This describes with

*An attractive
blue rat*

precision the requirements that an animal must fulfill and how it should look in terms of, for example, type, build, and color. Breed standards may differ from country to country. Not all the varieties of rat are universally recognized. Animals with noses that are too pointed, or that have tails with kinks, bald patches, or a poor condition will not score well when assessed. Furthermore, the breed standard includes a whole range of requirements relating to color and markings. Of course, as far as an ordinary house pet is concerned, it is not at all important if its blaze is slightly off-center, the eel stripe along its back is too short, or its feet are too white. Apart from show classes at competition events, there are often house pet classes you can enter, where rats are judged not on their appearance, but on how well they have been cared for, how well they can be handled, and their personalities.

The ideal rat

Build: strong, robust, and muscled, a good size

Body: females should be long and streamlined; males should be larger and arched over the loins

Head: long but not too pointed

Eyes: large, round, and bright

Ears: not too big, well formed, smoothly rounded

Tail: almost as long as the body, thick at the base, tapering gradually to end in a point at the tip

Coat: thick, smooth, and shiny; a slightly coarser structure in males than in females

---

The eyes are round and bright

3 CHOOSING AND BUYING A RAT

Not everything about rats is so great

Unfortunately, the following comments are quite common-place: "I'm looking for a good home for my three-month-old rat because, sadly, I just don't have time for it any more," or "We bought two rats yesterday, but it seems we're allergic to them, so they have to go." Cases like these show a lack of proper thought before purchasing a rat. Before you decide to buy, it is important for you to realize that, however wonderful rats might be, not everything about keeping these rodents is always so great.

• *Rats demand your time and attention*

Time is involved in daily care and weekly cleaning. Moreover, rats are social animals that regularly require their owner's more or less undivided attention. You have to arrange for someone to look after them when you go on vacation. At most, rats can be left alone for a long weekend, providing they are given sufficient food and water.

Rats require your attention

• Rats cost money

You have to invest in spacious, well laid-out accommodation and good quality food. If you are unlucky, you may have to deal with veterinary fees as well. Compared with other rodents, and partly because of their history as experimental animals, rats are fairly vulnerable when it comes to health and are particularly susceptible to skin complaints, respiratory infections, and tumors. You may end up paying veterinary fees that add up to many times the original purchase price.

• Rats leave their mark behind them

Rats are good at leaving tracks in the form of small droplets of urine, and they possess an unparalleled desire to gnaw on things. Above all else, they love to gnaw frayed holes in fabric,

Not everyone loves rats

such as clothing, the upholstery of the couch, or bedding. It is not possible to cure them of this behavior.

- **Rats can cause allergies**

Rats lose a relatively large amount of hair and flakes of skin in comparison to other small rodents, such as hamsters. This can result in respiratory irritations in people who are sensitive to this. When handling these animals, human skin is sometimes also affected by the scratching of rat claws, resulting in itching, red rashes, or bumps.

- **Not everyone is crazy about rats**

Some people are, and will always be, scared (phobic) of rats. So the presence of your animals will not always be appreciated everywhere. If someone in your family is panic-stricken by rats, it does not make sense to buy one.

• **Rats do not get on well with other house pets**
It is not a good idea to combine rats with other rodents and birds. In all probability, rats will pose a threat to their lives. Neither should you take any risks with ferrets, cats, or dogs; your rats will fall victim to their predatory instincts.

• **Rats do not live very long**
Sadly, rats have a relatively short lifespan. Many people manage to build a solid and, sometimes, very special relationship with their rats. Often, this makes having to accept their demise all the more painful.

Rats and children

Rats can be handled by children reasonably well and can be cared for with relative ease. Because rats enjoy interaction with their owners, children often get more from these animals than they do from other rodents. However, rats are not toys, and the responsibility for them should never be left to children exclusively. Children may well pester their parents incessantly for a rat, but once the novelty has worn off, it is the parents who end up having to care for it. So only decide to get

Black variegated rat

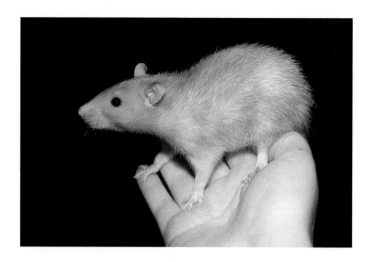

a rat if the whole family is in favor of the idea. Children between eight and ten, or under, should be allowed to handle a rat only under supervision. Furthermore, in the interests of the animal's welfare, you should always make rules about what is allowed concerning the rat and what is not: for example, always ask permission first before taking the rat out of its accommodation, do not go walking around with the rat, and do not let the rat outdoors.

Samuel Whiskers

The English children's book writer and illustrator Beatrix Potter (1866–1943) was probably one of the first children to have had a rat as a pet: her white rat Sammy, to whom she dedicated her children's book *The Tale of Samuel Whiskers,* published in 1908. She describes him as her "intelligent pink-eyed representative of a persecuted (but irrepressible) race. An affectionate little friend and most accomplished thief!"

Choosing a rat

There are a number of points to look for when choosing a rat. It is important for the rat to look healthy and show lively behavior once it is properly awake. When inspecting a rat, pay particular attention to its ears, coat, and breathing. If a rat has crusty skin on its ears or bumps on its tail, this may point to a skin infection. White or red specks in its coat may indicate skin parasites. Wheezing, rattling, or rumbling in an animal's breathing and/or a lot of reddish discharge from the nose or corners of the eyes are alarm signals for respiratory problems.

Dumbo rat with clean, full pink ears

A healthy rat:
- is active and curious;
- breathes regularly and not noisily;
- has perfect, clean, pink ears;
- has pink feet (not pallid, blue, or swollen);
- has a clean nose and eyes without any red discharge;
- has a clean, glossy, smooth coat;
- has a clean tail and anus (no traces of diarrhea).

Personality

Personality is extremely important. A rat that has not yet had time to get used to you properly will not always be keen to run along your arm and nestle on your shoulder straightaway. However, it should certainly not show extreme fear or be aggressive. Always choose a rat that likes to be handled. Each rat has its own personality, ranging from the lazy idler to the manic show-off. One rat may be very docile, while another may be slightly more dominant and require more work. Therefore, when choosing rats, spend plenty of time observing and handling the animals to get a better idea of their personalities.

Socialization

Socialization is extremely important in rats. Socialization means familiarizing the rat when young with everything that it might encounter in later life, such as other rats and people.

Each rat has its own personality

Young rats that have not had a proper opportunity to learn from their own kind, and have had too little contact with humans, often lag behind in the socialization process, and are able to catch up only with difficulty or not at all. Before transfer to a new owner, a rat must be sufficiently mature, strong, and, in particular, capable of handling stress. A rat is ready for this only at the age of four weeks at the earliest, and ideally you should wait until they reach six weeks. If an animal is too immature, it is still an unknown quantity.

A minimum of two

Housing a rat on its own is bad for the animal's well-being. Even if you were to devote two hours of every day to your pet,

Always get at least two rats

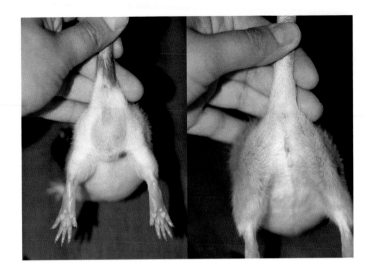

it would still be alone for the other 22 hours. A human being simply cannot substitute for the needs that a rat has for companionship. Rats are social animals that are at their most content with others of their species around them. They like to lie up against each other, play together, and groom each other. So you should always decide to get at least two rats. It will then become apparent how closely knit their lives are, how the order of rank is decided between them, and how they all develop their own personality. Do not worry that they will lose interest in you just because they are living together with others of their species. On the contrary, you will notice just how hard they beg for your attention! Rats that live alone can be more timid, insecure, withdrawn, and even aggressive. Rats feel more comfortable and gain more confidence due to the presence of other rats.

Male or female?

Both sexes make perfect house pets. Nevertheless, there are some general differences between males and females. Males are somewhat larger and heavier, and the older they get, the quieter and lazier they also often become. They can be unexpectedly dominant and feisty, particularly during their adolescence. Males often leave rather more urine markings, but females sometimes do this just as much. Females are somewhat smaller, lighter, and more slender; in their behavior they are more agile and active and, sadly, seem to be more susceptible to tumors. Identifying the sex of a rat is best done by looking at the distance between the anus and the genital opening: this is significantly wider in males than in females. In male rats, moreover, the scrotum is often clearly visible below the base of the tail. Specific names to differentiate between male and female rats do not exist in all countries. However, in the English-speaking world it is common to refer to male rats as "bucks" and female rats as "does," just as with deer or rabbits.

Where should you buy rats?

People usually buy rats from specialist pet stores or from hobbyists, who often advertise available animals. Some hobbyists specialize in rat breeding professionally and do this under the name of a "rattery" or "rodentry." You can find ratteries through rat clubs or the Internet. Another possibility when buying a rat is to get one from an animal shelter. Many animal shelters are full of abandoned rats that have nothing wrong with them and who are waiting longingly for a new owner. Quite a number of rats that wind up in a shelter, either sick or with behavioral problems, were originally bought from a pet store. Buying a rat from a store may come attached with a downside. The store might have purchased the animals from a wholesaler with a large-scale breeding program that does not concentrate on the personality, health, and socialization of the young animals as well as it should. Normally, a rattery knows the background of the rats that have been used for breeding, and you can usually inspect the parent rats as well. Hobbyists often devote a great deal of time to socializing and rearing young rats, and will be prepared to give you guidance and advice, even after purchase.

The difference in size between the male (right) and the female (left)

Good breeders pay particular attention to socialization

Whether you choose a specialist pet store or a rattery, there will always be some bad ones around of either sort. Unfortunately, no guarantees can be given for a healthy, long-lived rat. Wherever you decide to buy, always take a good look at the surroundings. Rats that are being kept together with too many animals in too small a space may be more susceptible to diseases as a result of the stress. Their accommodation must smell clean: do not feel shy about sticking your nose in to check! Note the type of cage litter used. If this is dusty, it might cause respiratory problems later in life. If you are buying a female rat from a group containing males and females enclosed together, there is a high risk of bringing home a mother-to-be.

Travel container
At the same time as buying your rat(s), also invest in a plastic travel container. A travel container is not only useful when bringing your rat home, but also comes into its own when visiting a veterinarian or a rodent show, or if you have to "stable" your rat when cleaning out its accommodation.

Getting started with rats
When first starting with rats, always choose either two males or two females. Otherwise, you are running a perpetual risk each month of ten or more rat pups being born. It is easiest to start with two or more young rats from the same nest. Two or more young animals from different nests can usually be put

together without any problem, provided that they are no older than about twelve weeks. Just because rats live communally and like to be surrounded by companions does not mean to say that you can always put rats together without thinking. Initially, rats will defend their territory fiercely against intruders, and newcomers are not always accepted without it first coming to blows. While placing older rats together usually works, there is an increased chance of problems arising because of the rats trying to achieve dominance. As a general rule of thumb, young rats under three months old adapt to each other most easily, while older males are the most difficult. And in general, the larger the group that a newcomer enters, the smoother the introduction. If you want to keep several rats, you can build up a group composed of different ages. The advantage of this is that your animals do not become old and die all at the same time. Four to six rats make a congenial little club. You could keep more rats, of course, but you should be mindful of the considerable amount of work that goes into accommodating and caring for a large group of animals.

Introducing new rats

Introducing new animals into an existing community must be done tactfully. You will need separate temporary accommodation for the new rat(s). The rats that you want to introduce to one another should be allowed to make each other's acquaintance a few times on neutral territory and under supervision. For example, you can get them to meet on the couch, the table, the bed, or, if you like, in the bathtub. The

Our territory

rats will then be primarily preoccupied with their surroundings and can slowly get used to each other's presence. If you anticipate problems, you can get all the animals to smell the same as each other by rubbing an identical scent into their coats—a drop of vanilla essence, for example. It is also possible to wash them before they are introduced; the rats will then be preoccupied with grooming their coats instead of taking notice of an outsider. Only once an introduction on neutral territory is going smoothly should you place rats together in the same accommodation. First, properly clean out this accommodation and give it a different layout so that it is new for all parties. Ensure there are enough hiding places to allow animals to withdraw and call time out. The cardboard cylinders from toilet or kitchen rolls can be put to good use as refuges for young rats; larger animals will not fit inside. Toys can provide distraction, but be careful about using tasty snacks to distract attention. This might, in fact, provoke a fight between the animals instead of providing the distraction you intended.

Determining order of rank

When newcomers enter a group, the rats will start to revise the order of rank that exists between them. The animals may chase after each other, compete against each other, or push each other onto their backs. It is often made very clear to young rats in particular that they must show respect to the older animals: they are turned on their backs rather roughly for a non-voluntary washing session. Be careful about introducing very young rats to a group. Make sure that the new animals are at least six weeks old and thus already capable of some self-defense. It may help to introduce not one but two animals at a time to the group. One can then act as support for the other, and the group's attention may be split between the two. These introductions can become a rather turbulent and boisterous business, but there is no need for you to intervene as along as no blood is spilled. Rats are usually able to resolve their own affairs quite well. Intervention can have the reverse of the effect intended: the lowest in rank may refuse to submit because he continues to receive your support. However, do not allow any incipient terrorization of an animal by others, and make sure all the animals can get to food, water, and their sleeping quarters. In some cases, attempts to get the animals to grow used to each other simply fail and sudden fights break out within the group. If so, you may need to remove the troublemaker from the group, either temporarily or for good. Remember never to put your fingers between fighting rats. Use a houseplant sprayer to separate them. A stream of water often startles them enough to stop and then start grooming their coats in order to get them back into shape.

On a journey of discovery

A rat will learn
how to get treats
from a food-
dispensing ball

4 HANDLING RATS

Getting to know your rat

Once you have brought a new rat home you will want to get to know it as soon as possible and immediately become best friends. However, be just a little patient on the animal's first day and give it at least twelve hours to explore its new accommodation. This allows your pet to feel safe and gradually get used to all the new smells and sounds. If you like, put a piece of material into the rat's cage that you have slept with the night before. This will soon familiarize the rat with your scent. If your rat comes from someone who has spent time socializing it, it is highly likely that your rat will walk up your arm of its own accord. If your new companion is still hesitant about making contact, you will have to gain the animal's trust by enticing it out of its cage with something tempting. Rule number one: never stick your fingers or hands into a cage suddenly! The rat may take your finger for a juicy carrot and take a bite, or be frightened by your hands hovering above it (like some bird of prey ready to swoop). Rats are territorial animals and can bite hard if they feel that they are being pushed into a corner on their own territory, or when they are disturbed in their sleeping quarters. Consequently, it is more sensible to let the animal come out of its cage in its own time. You could try tempting it out with a tasty morsel in a teaspoon. The advantage of this is that the rat cannot just snatch the food from your hands and you can entice the rat to follow after the spoon a little farther each time: first out of the cage and afterward onto your lap, or up your arm. Try to find out

Trust

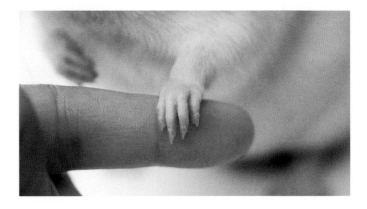

what your rat likes to eat most. If it shows no interest in the snack, you could remove the food from the cage for a couple of days. The rat will then have to come to you in order to eat. A rat that eats and grooms its coat in the presence of people is usually feeling relaxed. A rat that has become completely used to people will treat them more or less as though they were other rats. Some rats adore their "rat partner's" fingers stroking their cheeks, massaging them behind the ears, or tickling their bellies. There are even rats that will lie on their backs in complete abandon, reveling in all the attention. Then again, some rats are much too boisterous for all of that. If you really hit it off, it is more than likely that your rat will start to groom you, licking and nibbling you as it goes.

How to pick up a rat
Never pick a rat up either by its tail or the scruff of its neck. This is extremely uncomfortable and can even cause pain. It is best to hold a rat with both hands. Pick the rat up carefully, holding it with one hand from above just behind the front legs and with the other hand supporting the body from below.

Rearing

You will notice that rats go through different phases as they grow older. Between the ages of three and six months they are lively, playful adolescents still in the first flush of youth and inquisitive to learn about everything. At around six months of

age, rats start to work out their rank within the group and test out the limits of their status, not only regarding their rat companions, but also human beings. They must learn to understand and accept their place in the group. Males, in particular, can sometimes behave like petulant teenagers between their fourth and sixth months, and display dominant, macho behavior. You should then show your superiority as the "highest ranking rat" by turning an offending rat on its back and placing your thumbs on his chest to keep him in this submissive position for a short while. Adulthood lies between the ages of six months and one and a half years. A rat is fully grown in this phase and often becomes less boisterous. Rats are considered old from the age of one and a half. The likelihood of (age-related) ailments steadily increases from that time onward.

Young female black rat

Problem behavior

If a male keeps showing aggressive behavior toward people or other rats and has become unmanageable, discuss the situation with your veterinarian and consider having him castrated. Risks are attached to this course of action and thus it should not be carried out without good reason. Temporary, chemical castration by injection might also be worth considering. The rat concerned may even have calmed down by the time the effects of this have worn off, saving him an operation. For some rats, biting is not a show of dominance but one of pure fear, because they were not adequately socialized to get used to people. Rats that bite are usually the ones that have not been picked up very often. If you let go of a rat every time it bites, it soon learns that it can get its own way by biting. You must handle the animal all the more for precisely that reason. If you are scared that in so doing the rat will bite you, you could wear gardening gloves or scoop up the rat using a container. Gaining a frightened animal's trust requires that you give it a lot of attention, and it takes time. Ensure that you spend at least twenty uninterrupted minutes every day with the rat. Because a rat cannot remain continuously scared over such a long period, it will have to relax at some point. Keep hold of the rat, stroke it, let it walk over you, and make sure it cannot escape while doing so. You can also carry the rat along in a pocket or let it crawl into your clothing. Do not expect immediate results; to make progress you have to go very slowly. It may help to place a nervous animal together with a well-socialized rat that is curious and geared toward people. You do not need to worry that this will have the effect of making the well-socialized rat any less tame.

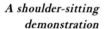

A shoulder-sitting demonstration

Castration: watch out!

If you are thinking of placing a castrated male in among one or more females, remember that it may still take a few weeks after castration for him to become completely infertile.

Sitting on your shoulder

Many rats will walk instinctively up your arm to your shoulder. It gives them a terrific lookout spot and, moreover, a warm place to nestle under your hair. Some people like to walk around with their rat perched on their shoulders, sometimes with a special safety harness. In so doing, remember that the rat needs time to do its business, eat, and sleep. So do not make these shoulder rides last too long.

Training rats

Rats are hugely intelligent, inquisitive, and enterprising. They enjoy being occupied and are always ready and willing for something new. It is possible to teach them all kinds of exercises. If your rat seems to have some talent, you can even teach it to carry things or to drop a mini-basketball through a rat-sized hoop. Swedish rat fanciers have come up with an obstacle course for rats including little high jumps, a seesaw, and slalom poles. Obviously, you will need your rat to trust you first before you can start on training exercises. The rat has to be happy about you picking it up, interested in tasty mor-

Always ready for something new

sels, and enjoy being given things to do. Having fun in doing things together is more important than the end result. There is no point at all in using force or administering punishment. Keep training sessions short; five to ten minutes is more than enough. Building up an exercise goes bit by bit, step by step. The speed it takes for a rat to master something depends less on its intelligence than on how good its owner is at making clear the point of the exercise!

Inquisitive...

Teaching exercises

Chapter Two mentioned the Skinner box in which rats discovered that they could obtain food by depressing a lever. Rats
that have learned to establish that connection depress the lever
more often. In other words, they will exhibit a type of behavi-
or more frequently if it provides them with a reward. You can
use this knowledge when training your rat: reward it each
time with some kind of treat if it does what you want. Timing
is of the essence in this. Reward the rat immediately it has
behaved as intended. Otherwise, you could be rewarding the
wrong behavior and the rat will not learn what you wanted to
teach it. At the right moment, reward your rat first with your
voice, and afterward give it a snack. Always use the same
words when giving the reward, such as "good boy," for example. After a few repetitions, the rat will soon latch on to the
fact that his behavior at the time he hears "good boy" is the
promise of something nice to eat. Keep these reward snacks
small; a rat soon fills up and is then not motivated to do anything for food. For example, you could give your rat a cornfla-
ke, a yogurt drop, or a husked sunflower seed, breaking these
treats up into much smaller pieces. Find something that your
rat likes best. Once the rat has fully mastered the exercises,
you can start to scale down the rewards, giving them only now
and then instead of every single time. The rat will continue
carrying out the exercises because, while it knows that a treat
will be forthcoming, it will not know precisely when. Get a
rat to perform an exercise a few times before attaching a command to it. If you simply say "jump" to your rat, it cannot possibly understand what you mean. With the aid of a treat, first
tempt your rat to perform in the particular way you want, and
afterward use the command at the moment that the rat actu-

ally does what you want: "Jump! Good boy!" Once the rat has grasped the idea, you can start issuing the command before the action, followed by a "good boy" and the treat.

Recall

Hold a treat in front of the rat's nose, say its name, and give it the reward. Next, hold the treat an inch or two farther away from the rat, obliging the rat to come to you to get it. In this way, you can start calling to your rat at ever-greater distances. Instead of using its name, you can also teach your rat to come at some other signal, such as rattling a can containing a treat. The rattling could act as a lifesaver in the unfortunate event that the rat escapes.

Teaching the rat to sit up

Hold a treat of some sort above the rat's nose and see whether this entices your pet to adopt the standing position you want. If it works, start to link a command word to the action, such as "up." By having your rat follow the treat, you can also teach it to turn round in a circle.

Creeping and slinking through

Teaching the rat to jump

You can get your rat to jump through a small hoop (or even a hoop improvised by your fingers). At first, get the rat to walk through the hoop a few times to reach a treat. Afterward, start to raise the height of the hoop just a little more each time. It is also possible to get the rat to jump from one object to another—a chair, for example. In that case, make sure that the landing surface is not smooth; otherwise the rat could just slide out of control. Increase the distance very slowly, literally inch by inch. This trick requires that your rat has a great deal of

Rope climbing

self-confidence! The rat can also learn how to jump onto your arm or chest, but do make sure that it does not perform this trick with people who are scared of rats. They are likely to get the fright of their lives and brush off the animal without a second's thought.

Teaching rope climbing

Secure a rope tightly to, for example, a table or a chair; anchor the bottom end of the rope using a brick or a heavy book to stop it from swaying about too much. Tempt the rat up the rope with a treat. Once the rat has grasped the idea, you can get it to keep climbing a little further each time before giving the reward. Take care that your rat does not fall!

Scent tracking

Show the rat a treat and then put it in the palm of one of your hands. Let the rat take it from you. If this goes to plan, start to close your hand a little more each time, until in the end the rat can tell which hand contains the reward only by smell. You can also play a "guessing game" using three plastic cups, hiding a treat under just one of them.

Teaching a rat to fetch and carry

Difficult, yes, but not impossible! Use a very small piece of material with a knot in it as the play object. The rat has to show interest in it at first; once he starts sniffing at it, reward him with a treat. Next, see whether the rat wants to take hold of or pick up the material. You might be able to make the rat do this by rubbing something tasty onto the material. Only once the rat picks it up of its own accord can you move on a stage by placing the object an inch or two farther away. If this also goes well, you can extend the distance covered a little farther each time. Hold a treat in your hand to entice the rat back to you with the object.

And now for my next trick...!

*Gnawing a
window for itself
in a box*

5 RAT ACCOMMODATION

A need for space

Fancy rats are robust, lively rodents that need a lot of space. As a general guide, housing two rats requires accommodation measuring at least 32 x 16 x 16 inches (80 x 40 x 40 cm). Height is as important as length and width, because rats typically stretch out upright on their hind legs in order to take in a thorough survey of their surroundings. Rat cages should always be kept out of the sun and placed in a well-ventilated, but draft-free, position. Rats are very interested in what goes on around them. Do not put them in a really busy area, but do put them where they can keep an eye on what is happening in their environment. Rats love climbing and clambering. For that reason, choose a roomy cage with horizontal bars and containing several stories. You can buy special wire cages for rats, but cages for chinchillas and ferrets, or an indoor aviary, may also be very suitable choices. Check carefully that the cage does not afford them any chance of escape. If a rat can get its head through a space, it can squeeze its body through as well. The cage must be made of gnaw-proof materials. Rats can even gnaw through hard plastic once they get a taste for it. Large plastic containers capped with a transparent roof, of a size to house guinea pigs and dwarf rabbits, are particularly

*A well laid out
wire cage for rats*

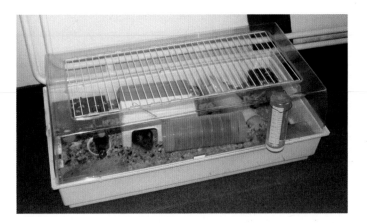

suitable for young rats before they reach maturity, because they might fall out through the bars or mesh of a wire cage. The disadvantage of these containers is that they are not so well ventilated and offer virtually no opportunities for clambering up the sides.

Do not house outdoors

Due to their sensitivity to the cold and drafts, fancy rats are not suitable for housing outdoors. The best temperature for keeping them is at around 68 degrees Fahrenheit (20 degrees Celsius) and at a humidity level of 50–60 percent.

Home-made accommodation

Rat fanciers are often very creative about joining together different cages or making their own rat shelters. Anyone who enjoys making home improvements can convert a bookcase or shelving unit into a rat palace. A bookcase with a height of roughly 5 feet 10 inches (1.8 m), a width of 31 inches (80 cm), and a depth of 14 inches (35 cm) can house up to seven rats. You can make the doors for the cage using wooden slats, wire mesh, hinges, and locks. The shelves can remain where they are, but you can cut passages through them to the other stories. You can fully personalize the layout of the unit with raised sections, suspension bridges, stairways, and even balconies or lookout posts secured with wire mesh. Use materials that are resistant to gnawing and free of any poisonous substances (such as paint). Doors must be large enough to allow

Two examples of floor litter: hemp litter (right) and wood chips (left)

you full access to the unit and any rat within.

Accommodation with smooth surfaces and the least amount of joins and corners is the easiest to keep clean. Raised edges prevent litter material from falling out of the unit. Placing a tray at the bottom of the unit makes cleaning even easier.

Spare accommodation

It is a good idea to have spare accommodation handy. This can come into its own if you need to house a sick animal temporarily, or if a rat has to give birth, or you have a new arrival that has yet to be introduced to the group. You can make your own spare accommodation using a large plastic container capped with a wire-mesh roof.

Litter and bedding material

Many rat fanciers use beech chips, aspen shavings, or hemp litter as litter material (although the latter is more easily available in Canada and Europe). Some also use recycled paper pellets or ground corncobs. These products are all fully absorbent and contain few substances to which rats might have an extreme reaction. Wood fiber is too dusty, and because of the rat's delicate respiratory system, you should also avoid aromatic litter material made, for example, from pine shavings and cedar chips, or anything impregnated with menthol. You must remember that any substance present in the air and breathed in by a rat is many times more concentrated for that animal than it would be for us. Experiments have shown that, when given the choice, rats prefer to avoid strongly scented litter. Rats love building nests. You can keep them happy with strips of cloth, non-printed paper, or white facial tissues, paper towels, and toilet tissue. Straw or hay can be used as well, as long as it is free of dust, insects, and mites. To be sure that your hay is free of pests, put it in the deep freeze for a while before use. Special nesting material can be bought from a pet store. Avoid using synthetic batting, as a rat can become entangled in this, resulting in the blood supply to its limbs being cut off. Printed newspaper is also unsuitable; the printing ink, which is toxic, can rub off onto fur and skin, or be ingested.

Cleaning

Rats are extremely clean animals. Unlike mice, they do not have a particularly strong body odor. However, they do produce urine that creates a strong smelling and, for the rat, harmful ammonia-laden vapor. If you can smell the ammonia, you are not cleaning often enough! Weekly cleaning is usually sufficient. You may need to clean their accommodation more frequently in warm weather, or if the animals have *Tubes are very* been eating lots of food with a high water content. If their *good for rat* accommodation starts to smell after only three days, you have *athletics*

too many animals living in too little space. Signs of overcrowding also include soiled coats, red discharge from the eyes, and fights between the rats. Do not only refresh the litter and bedding material when cleaning, but also clean the rats' accommodation and its contents with hot water and a mild detergent or, if necessary, an appropriate disinfectant. When necessary, wire cages can be cleaned under a shower or properly rinsed down with a high-pressure hose. The rats will not always be appreciative of your cleaning zealousness. The cleaner everything smells, the harder they will try to restore their own scent to their quarters by means of urine marking. A useful way of dealing with this is to put back a small part of the original bedding in the cleaned cage or box.

House-training
Some rats learn to do their business in a rat litter tray. You can set up one corner of their accommodation as a "rat bath-

A sheltered spot

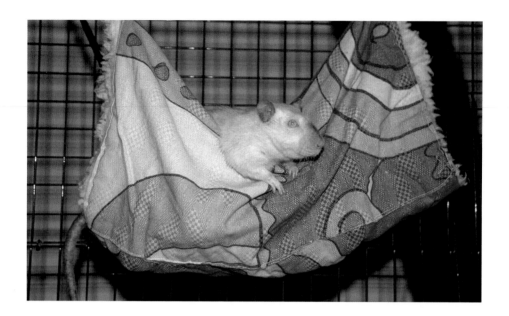

room," placing in it a shallow plastic container with dust-free or non-dust-making cat litter. Use a different litter material throughout the rest of the rats' quarters. To encourage the rats to use their tray, you could put some of their droppings or wet litter material into it. Some rats are easier to house-train than others, and some will urinate wherever they happen to be at the time, even in the nest box where they sleep.

Nest box

Make sure your rat has a quiet, sheltered spot in its home where it can withdraw. When deciding on a nest box, choose one that is roomy and easy to keep clean. The nest box must be well ventilated; condensation should not be allowed to form on the inside. Plastic nest boxes for guinea pigs or dwarf rabbits may be suitable. If you want a decorative bedroom for your rat, how about a big terracotta flowerpot? Your rat will also enjoy a cardboard box, through which it can gnaw its own doors and windows as it pleases. Rats love sleeping in hammocks or in suspended tubes, which can be bought in pet stores for ferrets. If you are feeling creative, you can make your own design using a few hooks, string, an old hand towel, or a leg cut off from a pair of jeans. Remember how much a rat loves to gnaw: given time, it may well gnaw its own quarters into pieces.

Rats love lying in hammocks

Rat athletics

You will be doing your rat a big favor by laying out its home so that it can perform its greatest hobby: rat athletics. If you search among the toys for larger birds at a pet store, you will come across wooden ladders and climbing ropes that are also suitable for rats. You can invent many other activity and playing ideas to keep your rats occupied. For example, rats enjoy collecting all manner of things together, such as balls of paper or dog biscuits, and then dragging them off to a secret storage place. They also love a cardboard box filled with toi-

In dreamland

let roll tubes in which you have hidden little snacks in balls of paper as treats. Using PVC tubes, you can make a series of assault course tunnels throughout the rats' home. From time to time, you can reposition the T-junctions, bends, and straight sections to create an entirely new construction. Regularly change your rats' exercising and playing equipment, always giving them something new to investigate.

Exercise wheels: the pros and cons

It is possible to put an exercise wheel in the rat cage, but its width and diameter must be great enough to allow the rat to run inside freely without being cramped. Choose a wheel with a solid back. A rat can risk getting its tail caught between open bars on the side, especially if one or more rats are using the wheel at the same time. Getting a rat to walk inside a plastic exercise ball is not at all animal-friendly. After all, the rat is not able to decide for itself whether it wants to be inside or not. Furthermore, the ball forces the rat to walk; it has only to lift a foot and the thing starts to roll off. Moreover, the ball could always split apart if the rat rolls hard against an object.

Allowing rats to run free

It is not sensible to allow rats the free run of your home.
There is too high a risk of them escaping, falling victim to a
larger pet, becoming stuck somewhere, or gnawing through
electric cables. If you want to create a "run" area in your
home, it has to be completely "rat-proofed" first. This means
no chinks or gaps through which to squeeze, doors and windows closed, no cables, no valued fabrics (such as cushions
and drapes) or antique furniture to gnaw on, and no house-
plants to nibble on (which may be poisonous). Whatever you
do, always keep your rat under supervision, because danger
often lurks in unexpected and seemingly insignificant places.

6 EATING AND DRINKING

Rats are omnivores

Rats, like people, are omnivores (eating both animal and plant matter). However, this does not mean that they may be allowed to eat everything or that they will eat whatever you give them. Wild rats are extremely cautious about new foods. "Tasters" carefully try out any unknown substance and the other rats will leave the food untouched if one of these tasters dies as a result. Being omnivores, fancy rats will also eat animal matter, such as meat, in addition to vegetarian food, such as grains. The idea that eating meat makes rats vicious is just an old wives' tale.

Basic food

Several brands of food can be bought that have been specially developed for rats. Ingredients typically used include grains, seeds, legumes, nuts, green vegetables, fruit, and meat. The manufacturers are not yet universally agreed about what the precise mixture should be for a rat. It is not just the ingredients that can be so variable, but also the percentages of proteins and fats, and the amounts of vitamins A and E. Too much or, conversely, too little vitamin A or E can be major factors in problems relating to skin and coat conditions or fertility. Therefore it is important to take this into account.

Various types of food are available

Two variants: mixed grains and rat blocks

Carefully check fat percentages if your rat has to go on a diet: one brand of food may contain up to three times as much fat as another. Unfortunately, there is no single best brand of rat food. Every rat is different and has its own tastes and needs. Choose the food that your rat enjoys and which it does well on. A large part of your feeding should be done by observation. Pay attention to your rats' coats (glossy and thick), their skin (not dry, irritated, or flaking), their weight (not too fat and not too thin), their appetite (good), their activity level (alert and lively, not subdued or hyperactive), and their droppings (no diarrhea).

Rat foods must

- be complete and contain all of the nutrients that a rat needs. Look for the word "complete" on the packaging;
- contain animal proteins. You can always complement food that contains no animal protein by using some dog biscuits;
- contain what your rat needs. Therefore look closely at their composition. Peanuts and sunflower seeds are fattening!;
- be fresh. Check the "use by" date. The packaging should tell you how best to store the product (usually somewhere cool and dry).

Mixed grain or rat blocks?

Rat food comes in two types: mixed grain, in which the various ingredients are visible, or rat blocks, in which all of the food has been compressed into pellets. The advantage of

mixed grain is that it gives the rat a somewhat more varied, more interchangeable, and thus probably slightly more natural diet. The drawback is that a rat can fish out the bits it likes most (with the risk of getting too fat on them) and leave the rest that it likes less. The advantage of rat blocks is that it removes the problem of any choosiness. Moreover, they guarantee that all your animals get the same level of nutrition and

If necessary, supplement their diet with dog biscuits

Enjoy your meal!

that the prime choices do not go only to the bossiest in the group; this matters if you have a couple of dominant rats. The downside to blocks is that it is rather dull food. Consequently, not all rats are wild about rat blocks. Ideally, serve meals in a glazed earthenware dish. It is gnaw-proof, simple to clean, and cannot be upturned easily.

How much?

According to manufacturers' guidelines, a fancy rat eats between approximately $^{1}/_{3}$ and $^{3}/_{4}$ ounces (between 10 and 20 grams) of basic food a day, depending on its needs and size.

Pregnant, suckling, and growing rats need more. Newborn rats weigh approximately one-fifth of an ounce (5 grams); a large adult rat weighs around a pound (500 grams). This means that a growing baby rat puts on one hundred times its initial weight in a very short space of time! As a general guide, a rat's diet should consist of 70–80 percent complete basic food, 15–20 percent vegetables and fruit, and 5–10 percent treats and rewards.

Supplementary food

Appropriate types of vegetables and fruit include chicory, broccoli, cucumbers, carrots, bell peppers, apples, pears, strawberries, and bananas. Keep an eye on "high water content" fruits; if a rat eats too much of these, it can quickly develop diarrhea. You can further supplement your rats' diet with pieces of meat and fish (for example, pieces of cooked chicken or cod, or a chicken bone, or a small can of complete dog food), yogurt or soft curd cheese or a little cats' milk, little pieces of mild cheese, bread crusts, rice, pasta (either cooked or raw), boiled egg, cornflakes, granola, nuts, birdseed (also sprouting), a spray of millet, and crackers. Keep quantities

Home-made rat nibbles

Not everything is
edible
small and remove leftovers promptly to prevent food from going bad. Specialist pet stores sell a wide range of special treats for rats. Yogurt drops are firm favorites for many animals. The addition of vitamin supplements and extra minerals is not necessary if a rat is being given a varied meal. You may risk overdosing your animals.

Recipe for rat nibbles

You can make your own hearty rat nibbles for your pets. You will need self-rising flour (9 ounces/250 grams), some granola (5 ounces/150 grams), an egg, and a few hazelnuts. Mix the flour, granola, and egg with a little water into malleable dough. You can use the dough to make cookies in the shape of rat ears, or else roll out long rat-tails, make little balls, or model an actual rat. Press the hazelnuts into the dough to give the rat some eyes or to decorate the cookies. Bake the nibbles in the oven for about an hour at 300 degrees Fahrenheit (150 degrees Celsius) until they are golden-brown and hard.

Taboo food for rats

Anything that is too salty, sweet, acid, fatty, hot, or spicy is not good for rats. Do not give your animals candy, such as licorice or chocolate, or snack food, such as potato chips. Raw beans, raw potato, onions, the green parts of carrots and tomatoes, blue cheeses, and types of cabbage that might cause bloat are also taboo for rats. This also applies to carbonated drinks: rats are unable to belch out the gas. You have to be extremely careful with sticky substances such as peanut butter that can cause a rat to choke and suffocate. Also be careful about the flowers and greenery that you bring indoors for decoration. Many garden plants are poisonous. Cows' milk contains lactose and can cause diarrhea. However, rats may drink soymilk, cats' milk (lactose-reduced), or yogurt.

Overweight rats

Male rats appear slightly more susceptible to becoming overweight than females. Depending on their type and build, males weigh on average between 10 and 21 ounces (300 and 600 grams); females average between 7 and 14 ounces (200 and 400 grams). Males weighing 24 ounces (700 grams) or more are burly fellows indeed, and females weighing in at 17 ounces (500 grams) are pretty hefty dames. Rats should not be

This rat is overweight

skinny, feeble, or bony; they should feel firm and robust. However, it is not good for them to be too plump, fat, or flabby either. An overweight rat must be put on a diet. Scratch treats, sunflower seeds, and nuts from its menu. If necessary, you can remove it from the group for a while if the other rats are getting high-calorie supplements or treats. While the other rats are eating, the dieting rat can be allowed to walk about under supervision for some extra physical exercise. Research shows that animals that eat too much fat and/or have a weight problem are more susceptible to tumors. Moreover, overweight rats run a greater risk of getting diabetes and have more respiratory problems. It is further speculated that a relationship exists between being overweight and symptoms of lameness in the hindquarters later in life. This should give you reasons enough to prevent your rats from becoming too fat!

Eating droppings
Some rats will eat part of their own droppings. This phenomenon is typical of rodents. The animals do this because the droppings still contain within them certain useful vitamins. It may look dirty, but it is nothing to worry about.

Exciting food

A ready-made meal from a dish becomes boring. You can put your rats to work by giving them exciting food that they really have to work for. For example, it is possible to put part of their meal in special food dispensing balls, available from pet stores for dogs and ferrets. The rat gets the food out of a slot in the ball by rolling it. You can further occupy your animals by hanging treats or gnawing objects high up in their container or cage (for example, hard dog biscuits). It is also possible to put their food in special (outdoor) bird feeders and hang these somewhere in their accommodation. Other ways to keep a rat busy are to get it to crack its own nutshells, peel its own boiled egg, or to extract food from a snail shell (that you have previously filled with, for example, a mixture of granola and canned meat).

Drinking

Compared with other rodents, a rat drinks rather a lot: approximately half a fluid ounce per quarter pound of body weight a day. Always remember to leave your rats enough fresh drinking water. It is easiest to use a water bottle. Clean it out regularly, and check that the tube still works properly each time.

7 HEALTH

Delicate creatures

Rat health can be quite delicate, particular where it concerns respiratory problems, tumors, and skin conditions. Unfortunately, not all rats live to a ripe old age; you may well get a rat that has nothing but problems. Some veterinarians specialize in treating rodents and have a great deal of experience in carrying out surgery and deciding on the appropriate course of (drug) treatment. Your local veterinary practice may be able to give you the address of a specialist veterinarian. You can also find out about specialists through other rat fanciers or rat clubs. Do not wait until your rat gets sick to do so!

Of critical importance for a healthy rat:
- clean and well-ventilated living quarters with enough fresh air (but not cold or drafty);
- a good diet;
- contact with other rats;
- enough physical exercise.

A healthy rat is full of life

An alert black rat

Off to the veterinarian!

It is important to be able to recognize symptoms early that might indicate a health problem. It is all too often the case that rat owners underestimate their animal's complaints and wait too long before getting medical assistance. A great deal of irrevocable damage may have occurred in the interim. So always visit your veterinarian if you think there is something wrong with your rat. Trying to play doctor on your own is foolish, particularly if experimenting with drug treatments. You are highly likely to give your rat the wrong dosage. The duration of treatment also has to be very precise. Consult with your veterinarian on how best to administer any drugs. For example, it is sometimes possible to make drugs more palatable by mixing them with vitamin C fruit syrup.

Medical information
Normal body temperature: approximately 100.4 degrees Fahrenheit (38 degrees Celsius)
Pulse: 250 to 500 beats a minute
Breathing: 70–150 times a minute

Health checks

It is sensible to check your rat's health every week, paying particular attention to the following:

1. Observe its behavior: is the rat lively or listless?
2. Check the toes and soles of the feet for injuries, swellings, or over-long nails.
3. Look at and smell the mouth to check for recently broken or missing teeth. Bad odor may indicate an infection.
4. Feel the body for any lumps or injuries.
5. Check the coat for bald patches, skin irritation, and signs of infestations.
6. Listen to the rat's breathing, which should be regular and noiseless.
7. Inspect the ears for irregularities, such as scabs or warts.
8. Check the eyes and nose for any red discharge.
9. Check the anus and vagina for any discharge, such as blood or traces of diarrhea.
10. Look at body posture. Alarm signals are an arched back, sunken flanks, a head held at a tilt, or a dragging foot.
11. Weigh the rat (use a kitchen scale), and record whether it is getting too fat or too thin.
12. Check the skin's elasticity by pinching a small amount of skin at the neck. If this ridge of skin falls back in place only slowly, it is a sign of dehydration.
13. Use your nose; the rat and its accommodation should both smell fresh.

Crusty skin may indicate health problems

Weight loss is often one of the first symptoms to indicate that there is something wrong with your rat. You should also see your veterinarian in the event of abnormal breathing, listlessness, blood in the urine, blood or some other discharge from the vagina, symptoms of lameness, major injuries, a sustained disinterest in food, loss of coordination, excessive scratching, continual diarrhea, bumps, cloudy, watery, or infected eyes, and symptoms of shock (such as a pale-colored mouth interior, feet cold to the touch, and staring eyes).

Help! My rat is crying blood!

There is something special about rat tears. A rat's eye contains the Harderian gland that secretes a reddish liquid called porphyrin. You will notice this substance around the rat's nose as well as its eyes. Many people conclude that their

A red discharge is visible in the corner of this rat's eye

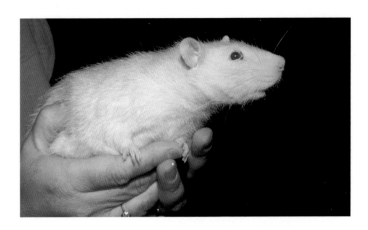

rat is crying blood, but that is not the case. This red discharge can be distinguished from blood under ultraviolet light, when it turns a fluorescent pink. The red tears are not an illness in themselves but do indicate that your rat might be feeling stressed or sick; a reason, therefore, for further examination of the animal.

Respiratory problems

Rats have a sensitive respiratory system. A respiratory infection often starts with sustained sneezing and a red discharge around the eyes and nose. Breathing becomes irregular and audible; the lungs start to rattle, wheeze, or rumble. Other symptoms are poor appetite, loss of weight, coarser, drier fur, and often a bent, arched back. The cause of a respiratory infection is usually a virus or bacterium that the rat will sometimes have carried around all its life, but which becomes active only in combination with stress and/or poor living conditions (dust, drafts, cold, and irritating substances such as cigarette smoke). Some bloodlines appear to be particularly prone to respiratory infections. Most respiratory problems are caused by *Mycoplasma pulmonis*, a microorganism closely resembling a bacterium that attacks the respiratory system. Left untreated, respiratory problems can lead to the development of a chronic condition and, in the worst cases, to pneumonia, resulting in death. Treatment often involves antibiotics, sometimes

Father and son

combined with a diuretic to reduce fluid in the lungs and decongestants to give the breathless rat more air. Rat fanciers sometimes use the common plantain (*Plantago major*) to alleviate breathing problems. It is possible to feed the raw leaf of this wild plant to your rat, if first cut up into small pieces, or to make a "tea" from it (let a level teaspoon of plantain leaf infuse slowly in 1 cup (250 ml) of hot water), which can be given to the rat to drink once it has cooled. Bromhexine hydrochloride can also be used as an expectorant to discharge mucus. Echinacea is used as a means of boosting the immune system, with varying results. These home remedies are useful up to a point, but do not overindulge in them. Respiratory problems really need to be nipped in the bud by taking proper action. The earlier you

Intrepid
Dumbo rat

start on a specific course of official treatment, the better the chances are of success.

Viruses

A variety of viruses can attack rats' airways. One example common in laboratory rats is the Sialodacryoadenitis (SDA) virus, which spreads quickly and can prove fatal as a result of subsequent opportunistic infections. Complaints appear after three to seven days: sneezing, which might include a running nose, dry eyes, and swollen lymph glands on the head. Animals become lethargic and may rub their eyes with their paws. There are still more viruses that can cause complaints symptomatic of bronchitis. Once a virus weakens a rat, this often opens the door to other infections, such as the *Mycoplasma* microorganism mentioned above. A rat that has recovered from a virus may continue to carry it in its body for months afterward. This is not something you can tell by its appearance. Viruses can spread easily through the air or on contact, such as at events where many rat fanciers meet. Anyone affected by a viral outbreak can be involved in a lot of suffering and high medical expenses. Consequently, never bring sick rats to gatherings, and always be careful when visiting places where many rats are assembled under one roof.

Quarantine

It may be sensible to keep new rats in quarantine for at least two weeks (to give any diseases the chance to reveal themselves), especially if you are not sure of their origins, before

Germs can be passed on quickly

bringing them into contact with animals you already have. This reduces the possibility of transmitting any germs and diseases. The best plan of all would be to house the new arrivals for a couple of weeks with someone who does not keep any rats. In any event, you must ensure that the new rats and old rats are kept as far apart as possible, in separate rooms. In your feeding, cleaning, and playing routine, always tend to your original rats first, and only afterward deal with the quarantined animals, subsequently washing your hands with antibacterial soap. Some rat fanciers even go so far as to shower and put on clean clothes. This may sound extreme, but it can prevent problems. Nevertheless, if you are unlucky enough to have a viral infection in your home, you should take care that your rats do not come into contact with the outside world for at least two months. Neither should you be breeding rats at this time—not for at least three months.

Tumors

Tumors can be either benign or malignant. Benign tumors are generally encased within tissue and thus are usually easy to remove. This is in contrast to malignant tumors, which often affect the tissues surrounding them. The appearance of lumps and bumps is a warning sign. However, cancer of the internal organs cannot be seen and often first makes its presence known only through weight loss and listlessness. Tumors can become very large in no time and even reach the size of a tennis ball, making the rat unsteady on its legs. For practical reasons, tumors should be removed as quickly as possible. Surgery is often successful, although a risk will always be attached to it, particularly because of anesthesia. However, some rats undergo several operations and come through without ill effect. Female rats are parti-

cularly susceptible to tumors. They are often afflicted by mammary tumors that develop between the forelegs or hind legs, or hang down from the belly. Mammary tumors are usually benign, although this is not to say that the animal does not suffer as a result of them, or that they do not cause any damage. To reduce the chance of rat tumors to a minimum, do your best to prevent your animals from getting too fat, and choose a male rat with the least possible tumors in its ancestry.

Surgery

Operating on a rat is complex, but it may be necessary sometimes in order to extend the animal's life. The advantage of an inhaled anesthetic for performing an operation is that it makes it much easier to control the precise level of anesthesia given, enabling the animal to regain conscious-

Surgery is sometimes necessary

ness quicker after surgery and significantly reducing the chance of death. Because rats are unable to vomit, they do not have to fast before an operation, unlike dogs or cats. A rat may eat and drink again after surgery, but only once it has fully regained consciousness. It is best to wait until the animal starts drinking again before offering any food. Make sure that its food is easily accessible and that the rat is getting enough liquids by giving it slices of cucumber. Proper hydration during and after an operation is vitally important. Rats lose body heat rapidly. Keeping them comfortably warm is very important both during and after surgery. You could put the rat on a towel or blanket, under which is placed a warm (not hot!) hot-water bottle. You could even use your own body as a kind of warming mat. Look for any loose bits of litter, because pieces of this could stick to the wound. Keep an eye on the rat to make sure it

Feeding with a syringe with a bulbous end

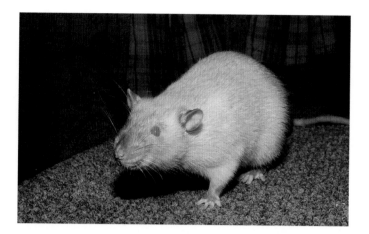

does not bite through into its wound. If necessary, protect the sutures by covering the rat in a body suit made from stocking. Deciding whether to keep a sick or post-operative rat in isolation depends somewhat on the situation. Separation from others might only cause it deep distress and do no good in helping it regain its health.

Special meals

You may need to adjust the meals you give to sick or convalescent rats temporarily. For example, you could supplement their diet with pots of baby food, canned kitten food, or babies' soymilk formula. You can make up a formula from these products that, if necessary, can be fed to an animal using a nipple- or tapered-tip feeding syringe (without a needle) or using a feeding syringe that has a needle with a bulbous end (i.e. with no sharp point that could cause injury). Do not feed too much rich food to the rat all at once, because its digestive system will not be able to process it. Build meals back up to normal gradually.

Abscesses

Abscesses are not tumors, as people sometimes mistakenly think, but infections that cause swellings due to a build-up of pus. If dirt gets into a relatively small scratch or bite wound, it can soon develop into quite a nasty abscess. An abscess often bursts of its own accord. Before it does, the skin on the affected area thins, turning red or darker. See a veterinarian if it fails to burst within two or three days, because the abscess is then likely to rupture internally, cau-

sing all kinds of harmful matter to enter the body. Never cut or puncture an abscess yourself. This might cause bacteria to enter the bloodstream and could prove life-threatening. It is important to squeeze out abscesses properly, wash them clean, and keep the wound open using ointment.

Skin problems

Skin problems can be recognized by itching, scratching, bald patches, redness of the skin, flakiness, crustiness, and small wounds. These complaints often build their own momentum: the rat starts to scratch, irritates its skin as a result, which makes the itching still worse, causing the rat to scratch all the more. The most common causes are parasites, an excessively protein-rich diet, or an allergy to something in the rat's food or environment. It might also be that a rat develops bald or short-haired patches in its fur as a result of "barbering," a behavioral term that describes rats grooming each other excessively. Lice and mites are the rat's most typical parasitic foes. Lice are often visible as red specks in the fur. Lice eggs, the nits, stick to the hairs in the form of tiny white granules. Lice infestations can be treated using a powder, spray, or shampoo. Ask your veterinarian for advice on what best to use, because not all preparations are suitable for rats. Mites are much more difficult to spot than lice. They hide in the fur or under the skin, where they cause terrible itching. The fur mite is hard to get to grips with because it lives in the skin. Rats in close contact, such as when in the nest, can pass the parasite on to each other. There need not be any visible external signs, but once

Chocolate rat

a rat's immunity levels drop because of, for example, stress or poor hygiene, the fur mite may start to take advantage. Typical signs of fur mite infestation are cauliflower ears and bumps on the tail. However, frantic scratching may equally be the only symptom that you see. Ivermectin is a useful agent against mites, often administered in the form of an injection or spray. Several treatments are usually necessary when ridding an animal of parasites. In addition, you should not forget to treat the rat's accommodation as well, including litter material and the other animals.

Nail clipping

Rats with long, sharply pointed nails can injure their skin during daily grooming sessions, especially in areas just behind the ears and on the neck. This is why it is important to keep nails short, particularly those on the hind feet. Place

Black husky

a rough stone or brick in the cage to help the rats wear down their nails, forcing them to use it by positioning it, for example, under a water bottle or below the entrance to another story. You can also use a small pair of nail scissors or clippers to clip away sharply pointed nails carefully. When doing this, do not cut into the living nail bed, indicated by a pink color. Nail clipping is easiest with two people: one to hold the rat and the other to do the clipping.

Bathing a rat

Rats groom themselves to keep clean; their fur needs little maintenance. Only give a rat a bath if it is really necessary, because washing is a stressful experience for the animal and is not all that good for its natural skin condition. It is easiest to fill a sink or basin with warm water. A rat's body temperature is slightly higher than ours; what we feel as lukewarm might be just a little too cold for the rat. Keep its head above the water and remember that the animal may try to resist. Carefully, make the rat wet, and wash it with a mild baby shampoo or one especially for animals. Properly rinse off the suds, and carefully dry off the rat. If necessary, use a soft toothbrush to remove any brown accretions on the rat's tail. The fur, particularly in older male rats, can become rather greasy, orange-yellow in color, or crusty as a result of overactive sebaceous glands (a condition known as seborrhea). If your rat is really irritated and itching because

Ready to go out scouting

of this, wash it using a special shampoo available from your veterinarian.

Rat teeth

Rat's incisors continue to grow throughout their lives. This happens at quite a rate: several inches a year. The incisors wear down through contact with each other (bruxing). If the upper and lower incisors are not properly aligned, they may start to grow past each other. There is no point in giving rats additional material to gnaw on in this instance; the teeth simply cannot abrade each other because of being incorrectly positioned. This causes "elephant tusks" to appear, which can grow out of the mouth or even through the roof of the mouth. This prevents the rat from being able to eat properly. It may start to salivate and will lose weight rapidly. In such cases, the teeth must be clipped regularly. At first, this should be a job for your veterinarian. The rat can be held fast rolled up in a towel to prevent accidental cutting of the tongue or lips. A broken tooth will grow back of its own accord. Make sure that the tooth opposite does not become too long in the interim, and supplement the diet with soft food if the rat is undergoing temporary problems with gnawing. Rat teeth are not in fact radiant white but orange-yellow. It is normal to find some gap between the lower incisors, causing them to grow apart from each other slightly.

Bumblefoot

Rats may suffer from bumblefoot, an infection of the heel often caused by walking on hard surfaces or wire cage floors. This infection, which can be treated with antiseptic ointment, but which heals with difficulty, usually appears on both hind feet. The soles become red and swollen, often forming a crusty scab. Heavier rats are particularly susceptible to this. Bumblefoot can be prevented by keeping your rats' accommodation clean, preventing them from becoming overweight, and covering hard surfaces and wire floors in a soft or canvas material.

Ear problems

Head shaking and scratching the ears may indicate an infection of the outer ear. If so, the ear is often painful, dirty, and irritated. If a rat is also tilting its head to one side and is having trouble keeping its balance, it might be suffe-

Too much food with a high water content can cause diarrhea

Adjustments to a rat's diet are sometimes necessary

ring from a middle-ear infection that could spread to the inner ear. This could leave the rat with permanent impairment of its hearing, a crooked head, and even meningitis. In the event of ear problems, always see your veterinarian to get specific treatment.

Intestinal disorders

Diarrhea is often caused by stress, a change of diet, or overfeeding animals vegetables with a high water content. Contact your veterinarian if diarrhea persists. It is important for a rat suffering from diarrhea to be getting enough liquids inside it. One way to combat dehydration is with ORS (oral rehydration salts), a soluble powder available from pharmacies containing all kinds of essential minerals. Megacolon is a congenital disorder that prevents the intestines from functioning properly. Food either passes through the intestines undigested, causing the animal to die of starvation, or else blockages occur in the intestines, eventually bursting through and resulting in a painful death. Megacolon can be first identified fairly soon after birth through retarded growth. Although they continue to drink, the baby rats fail to put on any weight. The second sign is the development of an extremely distended belly due to the blockages and swellings in the intestines. In most cases, megacolon results in euthanasia at a young age. In rare cases, it is possible to keep animals alive on a diet of easily digestible and extremely juicy food with a high water content, such as melon, pears, and baby food.

First aid

The same applies to accidents as applies to illnesses: if the injury is severe, or if you are in any doubt, then instead of trying to play doctor, go straight to your veterinarian. In general, wounds caused by bites heal pretty quickly; it is not usually necessary to suture or cover the wound. The veterinarian will wash and disinfect the skin, perhaps treating it with an antiseptic ointment. As a temporary measure, you should then put down face tissues in your rat's quarters instead of loose litter, which could stick to the wound. A bruised foot generally heals if given rest. Swellings can be treated using a cold compress, possibly combined with an appropriate painkiller. Unfortunately, not a great deal can be done about broken bones. A broken leg usually heals by itself, but will often leave a visible bump behind.

Do not try to play doctor when accidents happen

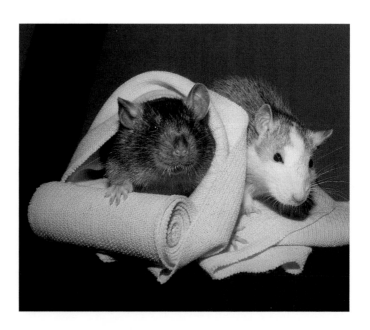

This rat is overheating

Poisoning

If your rat has eaten something toxic, give it activated carbon to absorb the toxins in the stomach. Rats are unable to vomit, so there is no point in trying to make them bring up anything that way. Take the animal to your veterinarian as soon as possible.

Overheating

Many rats succumb to overheating every year. Temperatures in plastic or glass aquarium containers can rise unnoticed and at lightning speed, with fatal consequences. If a rat is lying outstretched on its back away from its bedding, you should assume that it is overheating. Drowsiness, wheezing, accelerated breathing, damp fur around the genitals, and slobbering at the mouth indicate that something is seriously wrong. You should take an overheating rat straight to a dark, cool, and quiet area, and slowly cool it down using cold, damp towels. Get your veterinarian involved immediately, because this is an emergency. Rats drink more during hot weather and, therefore, also urinate more. Be additionally scrupulous about hygiene and ventilation because of this. If it becomes extremely hot, there are various ways you can provide additional cooling, which include hanging a cold, damp towel over one side of the cage. Never cover the entire cage, because this causes excessive humidity and will have a counterproductive effect. Another possibility is to half-fill a plastic bottle with water, freeze it, and then rest it on or against the rat's housing. You can also help your rats by giving them a slice of frozen banana, a cube of frozen yogurt, or a rat "Popsicle"

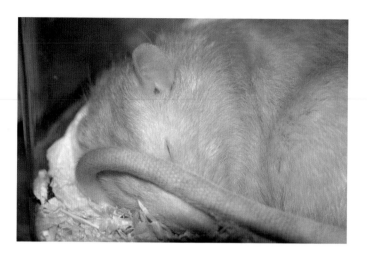

in the form of an ice-cube containing a few drops of vitamin C fruit syrup. Always wash frozen products under the faucet with lukewarm water before giving them to rats, otherwise their tongues or feet could stick to them. Too much in the way of cold food may cause irregularities in the digestive system. You could put frozen peas or other pieces of fruit and vegetables in a dish filled with water to get the rats to fish them out. Swimming should always be a rat's free choice. If you like, put down a bowl of water and let the rat decide for itself whether or not it wants to get its feet wet.

Old age

Research shows that, on average, wild rats generally live no longer than a year. Fancy rats rarely live much longer than two to three years. Three years is a good age, although far from all rats manage it. The record for the oldest rat appears to stand at over seven years, but that is truly exceptional. Older rats need rather more looking after. They become slower, thinner, and lose their condition. They may have more difficulty moving because of weakened or lame hind limbs. Their general health often deteriorates as a result of lung, heart, or kidney problems. Make sure that older rats have easy access to everything in their quarters. For example, you could put the nest on the lowest level of the accommodation and use a shallower dish for feeding, containing softer food. Their fur and fat reserves often become a little depleted causing them to feel a chill more easily, so ensure that they have enough bedding to lie in.

Old rats that are no longer able to groom themselves well can be washed carefully using a damp face cloth.

Accepting death
When there is no longer any hope of lessening an animal's suffering, it has used up too much of its reserves, and has lost all its zest for life, you have to prepare to say farewell. The veterinarian can put the rat to sleep. Some methods are more painless for rats than others. The best type of euthanasia is to anesthetize the animal with gas, followed by a fatal injection, usually administered to the heart. Ask your veterinarian specifically to anesthetize the animal in advance, because this may not always be their standard procedure. In order to grieve for the death of an animal, it often helps to make a photo album, web page, or poem, or place or plant something special in the garden as a remembrance of your pet.

This rat's sunken flanks betray its old age

8 BREEDING RATS

Think twice...

You may have become such an enthusiast that you want to start breeding your own litter of rats. However, you should think twice before you begin, and do not underestimate the work involved in rearing the litter. It takes up a lot of your time to socialize and care for baby rats—referred to sometimes as kittens (and as pups in the scientific community). The birth of a litter usually goes well, but, occasionally, it can also go wrong, resulting in the loss of the young or even the mother. With each delivery, a rat can easily bring 10 or more babies into the world, all of which have to be found new owners. With that in mind, you could put up advertisements in a pet store, at the veterinarian's practice, or at your local supermarket. However, you may get 15 rat babies just at a time when there seems to be little interest in rats, or when the babies' coloration is not in fashion. Moreover, you cannot simply shrug off your responsibility when you are the breeder. Are you prepared to take back an animal bred by you if the owner no longer wants it? And what if the owner should knock on your door because your breeding "product" appears to have a health "defect?" Before you start on breeding, it makes sense to keep rats for a few years first and really get to know all about these rodents. It is often quite possible to make inquiries with an experienced breeder first through rat clubs and associations. Many breeders are quite happy to help

Birth

You can already tell from their eyeballs that these baby rats will have dark eyes

a beginner, not only in terms of their knowledge, but also in terms of seeking out the right parent animals and finding homes for the litter. Unfortunately, the special animal refuges for rats that have appeared are full of examples of how that should not be done. Prevent the rat from becoming a victim of its own success. These cute, long-tailed creatures do not deserve that fate!

Rat reproduction
Sexual maturity: from the age of 5–6 weeks
Fertile: once every 4–5 days
Gestation: 21–24 days
Number of young: 2–20, usually 8–12
Birth weight: averages one-sixth of an ounce (5 grams)

The skin starts to develop pigment at approximately day three

The parent animals

Not all rats are suitable for breeding. Only use parent animals for breeding if they are healthy and always have been, if they have good personalities, and if their weight is normal. Do not breed with rats if they have been treated for respiratory disorders or have had surgery for tumors, if their immediate ancestors have had health problems, or if they are aggressive, timid, or unfriendly. It is also best not to breed with animals that are closely related. Interbreeding can result in symptoms of degeneracy (such as animals that are too small), decreased fertility, and congenital defects. Inbreeding is not the cause of hereditary defects, but is more likely to bring to the surface any hereditary defects that are already present in the rats' genes. A female must weigh at least $10^{1}/_{2}$ ounces (300 grams) to have a litter and must be at least four weeks old, preferably five. She should not be older than 8 to 10 months if it is her first litter. If a rat is any older, her pelvis will have fused together and no longer be as supple, which can result in serious problems during the birth of a first litter. A female that has already had a litter can continue delivering young up to the age of 12 or 14 months. After giving birth, you should give females plenty of time—some three months—to recuperate. Before she can be mated again, she must regain the body weight she had at the time of the first mating at the very least. Three litters for a female is really the maximum; any more births would be bad for her health. In contrast, a male can mate throughout his life from the moment that he becomes sexually mature. However, many rat breeders wait

Coloration and markings become increasingly defined at approximately day seven

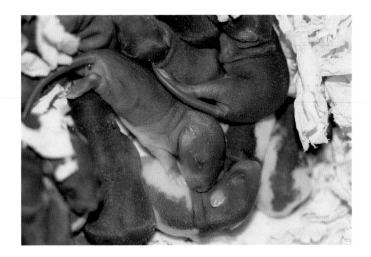

until a male is a year old or more before putting him to stud. The advantage of this is that by that time his character will be fully formed and more will be known about his health. Little is yet known about any possible adverse effects from using very old (or, conversely, very young) males to father offspring. If a male rat mates when six months old and still in adolescence, it can cause dominance tensions to surface within his social group. Always bring the female to the male and not the other way around. The male might otherwise react aggressively when brought home again.

Mating

If you do not have a male rat of your own, you will need to start looking for a suitable partner for your female. Some rat fanciers, and virtually all breeders, will make their rats available as "stud rats." The female is fertile for a few hours every four to five days. She will often be more active and lively at this time. To see whether a female is ready to be mated, it is best to place her next to the male. A female ready for mating will stiffen her movements in front of a male, lie flat on her belly, hollow out her back, and vibrate her ears. The male then proceeds to mount her several times, taking a number of breaks in between to give himself a thorough grooming. If mating does not occur immediately, let the male and female stay together for ten days, or less if you have witnessed mating take place. All being well, the female should become fertile twice during this ten-day period, and therefore you have two mating oppor-

tunities. Meanwhile, it is sensible to return both animals regularly to their own groups for a brief period to prevent them from becoming alienated from their rat companions. If a female reacts very aggressively to the presence of a male, it is better not to get them to sit together and simply to try it again later. If the male and female stay together after mating, you must, nonetheless, remove the male shortly before the birth. This is because the female can become fertile again and mated within a day of delivery! Be careful about leaving males and females together if you do not want any babies. Mating requires only a few seconds; before you know it you could end up with a, perhaps, not-so-happy accident.

Almost two weeks old, and their eyes are still not quite open

Over two weeks old: we can see!

Gestation

An increase in weight, confirmed by using a scale, indicates that the mated female is pregnant. Ensure that a gestating rat has enough food—after all, she may have to eat enough for ten or more. Only in the final days before birth does the mother develop a clearly visible, distended belly. The female then also gets the urge to build a nest. You should give her accommodation a thorough clean and provide sufficient nesting material, such as strips of face tissues. Some rats use this to build nice round nests; others prefer to build a flatter environment for a nursery. Allowing the rat to give birth in its sleeping nest is awkward; you will not be able to inspect the nest properly. Some rat breeders let the gestating female give birth within the group where she lives. Other females can then become "aunts," playing a role in

The first forays and feeding outside the nest

rearing the litter, but make sure that the mother rat has enough privacy and that the other females do not become a disturbance factor, by stealing kittens, for example. You can also choose to isolate the mother-to-be shortly before the delivery. This is particularly necessary in the case of a low-ranking female in the group, since the dominant female may otherwise snatch away the kittens. The accommodation in which the rats are to be born must be one suitable for rearing kittens. These tiny creatures can easily fall through bars or wire mesh.

Birth

Rats are generally born at great speed. The mother rat does everything herself: she breaks open the birth sacs, bites through the umbilical cords, eats the placenta, and licks her young clean and dry. Leave her to do this in peace as far as is possible. The faint squeaking of the kittens will be audible once birth has become a reality. Leave the litter alone for the first day, and on the second day look carefully to see whether everything is as it should be. Any dead kittens can be removed during this first inspection. Before handling kittens, you should rub your hands first with some of the nesting material to avoid altering their scent too much. Some rat mothers will protect their young with a startling ferociousness, even when they are normally as sweet as can be. Be aware of this. The best thing to do is to distract the mother's attention briefly by enticing her with a treat.

Complications

Complications may arise during birth. The delivery might be held up, perhaps because a kitten is stuck in the birth canal and the female is only losing blood. If so, you need to call your veterinarian immediately. Sometimes, a female will eat one or more kittens. In most cases, this involves stillborn or deformed kittens. A mother rat that is extremely stressed may ignore the litter or start dragging her kittens about. As a temporary measure, it may then help to place mother and young together in a very small container. If the worst happens and the mother rat dies, you are landed with a big problem. The best thing to do is to find another female with a litter of the same age as soon as possible. With luck, the orphans may be incorporated within her litter. The chances of successfully rearing immature rats by hand are extremely small, especially if the kittens

Rush hour at the feeding bowl; the litter is now three weeks old

are less than two weeks old. It is not easy to keep the litter at the right temperature using heated mats and warm hot-water bottles. Very young, motherless rats must be fed every two to three hours, day and night. Milk substitutes commonly used include goats' milk, special formulas to rear young dogs or cats, or soy formula for babies. Feeding should be done at the same time in very small doses using a very small bottle, a plastic feeding syringe, or even an absorbent fabric on which the kittens can suck. In the first

At four weeks: still sleeping under mother's guard

week following delivery, you can get a good idea of whether an animal has been taking in its milk or not from the translucency of the kittens' skin: a yellowish-white patch should be apparent at the spot where the stomach is. After feeding, the baby rats' stomachs need to be very gently massaged to help keep their bowels moving; use warm, damp cotton batting or a Q-tip for this. You can gradually move the kittens on from milk to pap as soon as their eyes open, feeding them at first with your finger.

Development

Young rats develop with lightning speed. Kittens are hairless at birth, and their eyes and ears are still closed. You can tell the sex of an animal immediately after its birth by the distance between the anus and the genitals. It is also possible to tell their eye color. If the area covering the eyeball is dark, the rat will have dark eyes. If that spot is pink, it will be a red-eyed rat. At around the third day following its birth, a rat's skin starts to develop pigment, showing whether it will be colored and how it will be marked. The tiny ears slowly begin to emerge on the head. At around day seven, coat color can be discerned clearly, and the kittens start to crawl. At around day ten, the kittens become increasingly active and mobile. Very small teeth start to break through. The babies' weight will have quadrupled since their birth; their average weight is now just under one ounce (between 20 to 25 grams). The eyes start to open around day fourteen. From that time onward, the kittens start to stray ever further from the nest and begin eating solid food. You will still be able to tell the sexes apart easily

Canned food eases the transition to dry food

Make toys varied, and provide lots of them

because their bellies are not yet densely covered in fur. Rows of nipples will be clearly visible in females. The young rats will now be getting increasingly inquisitive about their environment, leaving the mother rat with her paws full in retrieving wandering kittens and keeping her brood together. By the time she has number eight in her mouth and has brought it back to the nest, the first seven will have often gone off scouting again.... By the age of three weeks, the kittens will have grown into fully formed little rats. However, they are ready to live independently only once they reach four weeks of age—and, ideally, six weeks.

Rearing rats and socialization

During the first week of life, it is the mother rat that takes on most of the work. There is not much for you to do concerning the litter at that time. Pick up kittens with care only to check them over; this gets them used to being handled. If the mother becomes very agitated about your presence, it is better to leave the litter alone for the time being. It is easier to handle the kittens once they are two weeks old and have opened their eyes. To ease the transition from mother's milk to solid dry food, and to minimize the possibility of constipation, you can supplement the kittens' feeding, if you so wish, with a some kind of pap, starting from week two to week three. For example, this could be canned food for (feline) kittens or grains mixed with soymilk. If you do this, remember that *supplementary* food is supple-

mentary only and it should not become the rats' main meal. The period between the second and sixth week is of crucial importance for socialization and is the optimum time for getting young rats used to the presence of humans. To achieve this, you should handle the kittens for a while each day, and talk and play with them. Do be careful doing this, because these young creatures are still extremely delicate. Be extra careful picking up rats aged around three weeks, because they are then in what rat fanciers call the "Ping-Pong ball stage" and can suddenly jump out of your hands without warning! Too much handling and too little opportunity for rest can make the animals stressed and more vul-

At five weeks: almost time to fly the nest

nerable to illnesses. Young rats need space. Make sure they
have lots of different things to play with to help them find
out as much as possible about the world around them.
Contact between litter companions is very important. You
will notice how the kittens use each other to act out all sorts
of behavioral situations. This is preparation for living and
dealing with other rats later in life. All of these rat "tod-
dler" antics are enormously entertaining.

On their own four feet

Since rats can be sexually mature as soon as the fourth week
of life, it is sensible to separate male kittens from their sisters between the fourth and fifth weeks. Let them grow up
in two groups until they are six weeks old: a group of brot-
hers and a group of sisters, who can still be with their mother from time to time. As a general rule, young rats are able
to live independently "on their own four feet" and go off to
new owners once they are at least five weeks old and weigh
at least 2^1/$_2$ ounces (75 grams). By now you will be well
aware that rats are communal animals. Therefore, ensure
that a new owner does not keep a young rat alone. If a new
owner does not have any other rats, many breeders will only
sell their babies in pairs.

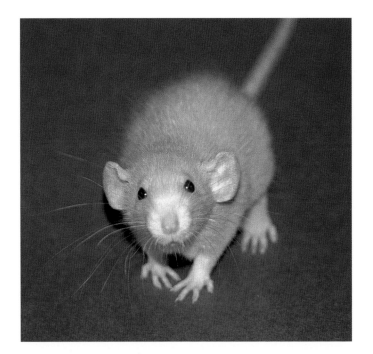

The value of a pedigree

Many rat fanciers issue their rats with a pedigree. This is a document that contains information about the rat itself and its ancestors, such as names, colors, and birth data. Breeders compile their own pedigrees and, consequently, they are not official documents and offer no guarantees. A rat with a pedigree is not per se better or healthier than a rat without one. However, a pedigree does indicate that a breeder has taken the trouble to research the background of his or her rats and takes breeding seriously. If you want to breed from your own rat, a pedigree can be important in finding out more information about its ancestors.

9 COLORS
AND VARIETIES

Color conformation

Over a hundred years ago, black rats and pink-eyed white rats (albinos) appeared alongside agouti rats at the first rat shows in England. The familiar hooded rat, with its colored head, neck, and shoulders, and stripe along its back, is also a very old variety. In 1976, when the National Fancy Rat Society was founded in England, there existed in addition to the original agouti rat only five other varieties: pink-eyed white, silver fawn, black Berkshire, and hooded. Now, dozens of different colors and marked varieties have been recognized, the names and descriptions of which may differ from country to country. This chapter does not claim to be exhaustive. Instead, it provides an overview of the most typical varieties of color, markings, coat, and physical appearance that occur in rats.

Trends

Rat colors are subject to the latest trends. New varieties, in particular, are often extremely popular. Thus rat fanciers fly into an immediate frenzy as soon as the word is out about an innovation. Examples of this are the incredible excitement that began in the mid-1990s over the husky (roan) rat—a rat with markings similar to those of its

The "original" agouti (wild-colored) rat

*Fawn rat with
black eyes*

namesake, the husky dog—and the blue rat. Large-scale breeding programs were begun to meet the great demand, which was of no benefit to rat health. Many animals turned out to be rather weak, susceptible to illnesses, and short-lived. Behavioral problems were also noted. People should realize that a rat is more than a color. It is the animal as a whole that matters.

Colors
Agouti (wild-colored)
Agouti is a mixture of chestnut brown, gray, and black and originates from the coloration in the wild. The hairs are banded dark gray at the base and black at the tips. These flecked hairs, with their different bands of color, are referred to as "ticking." Entirely black guard hairs are also found in between. Agouti rats have paler, silver-gray bellies and dark-colored tails. Their eyes are black.

*Pink-eyed
white rat*

Cinnamon
Cinnamon rats have warm, pale-chocolate coats with darker, russet-brown tips. The belly is a pale agouti; the eyes are ruby or black.

Fawn
Gradations of fawn rats may be described under a variety of names, such as apricot agouti, argente, fawn agouti, orange, silver fawn, and topaz. The color ranges from a mixture of fawn and silver hairs to a rich golden orange. The eyes may be black, red, or ruby.

Black
Black rats should be as solidly black as possible and, ideally, should not have any paler hairs or white feet. Eye color is black.

Chocolate
Chocolate rats are an even dark chocolate-brown. Their eyes are black.

Champagne
An even, warm pale beige with a pinkish cast, neither too yellow nor too gray. They have red eyes.

White
The ideal white rat is as pure white as possible without any creamy tinges or markings. Eye color may be bright red (pink-eyed) as well as black (black-eyed).

Blue
There are various types of blue rat with colors ranging

Mink rat

from bright sky-blue to dark slate-blue. The Russian blue rat has the same very dark slate-blue color as the blue Great Dane, the Russian blue cat, and blue British short-haired cat, and has black eyes. There are additional varieties, such as the sky-blue rat (between blue and powder-blue: a clear sparkling blue), the blue agouti rat (a medium slate-blue "undercolor," blue guard hairs, silver-blue belly), silver blue rat, and platinum rat (an even dove-gray with ruby eyes).

Mink and lilac
Mink and lilac are colors that closely resemble each other. The mink rat is an even mid-gray-brown with a bluish sheen and has black eyes. The lilac rat is a medium dove-gray evenly mixed with brown and has ruby or black eyes.

Rats can turn rusty!
Rats' coats can change color slightly as rats get older and become browner. The appearance of these brown tinges is known as "rusting."

Markings
Variegated
This description includes a variety of marking types. Ideally, the "regular" variegated rat should have markings distributed over its whole body as evenly as possible and a white patch on its head. Variegated rats with very small

Hooded rat with ideal markings

splashes of color on their bodies are called Dalmatians. There are also white animals that only have markings on their heads, ranging from "masked" (a colored mask around the eyes) or "capped" (a colored cap on the head not extending to the throat or past the ears) to "blazed" or "badger" (a white wedge-shaped blaze on the face from muzzle to ears).

Irish rat

The Irish rat is completely colored with four white feet and a distinctive white marking on the chest between its forelegs. Depending on the breed standard, this can be a white triangle (the apex of which points toward the tail) or a round white patch.

Berkshire

The Berkshire rat is a colored animal with a large white marking on its belly. Depending on the breed standard, this marking may range from a white triangle on the belly to a completely white underside. A distinctive feature of many Berkshire rats is the half-colored tail and the white spot or blaze on the head (then called a blazed Berkshire or badger).

Hooded

The hooded rat is white with a colored head, neck, and shoulders and a colored eel stripe running down its spine, which, ideally, should be unbroken and as evenly aligned as possible and must run on down to the base of the tail.

Merle rat

Hooded rats that only have head markings and lack an eel stripe are called bareback rats.

Downunder
The downunder is a rat whose markings are visible on both its back and its belly. This can include a stripe (in the case of a hooded rat) or splashes of color (in the case of a variegated rat). The downunder's name derives not only from its underside markings, but also because the variety was discovered in Australia.

Merle
Merle rats have patterns of small dark splash-spots of color on a lighter background. The markings are not always easy to see.

Husky (roan)
The husky rat has markings similar to those of the husky dog after which it is named. It is characterized by a white belly and feet, a white blaze on its head, and intermingled colored and white hairs on its back. Its markings show up best when combined with darker colors, such as black. Show animals should have a level blaze, a clearly demarcated line between colored areas and white, and the right degree of color intermingling.

Is it a husky... or isn't it?
The husky is a very popular variety; its charming white blaze and distinctive color combination captivates many people. However, there is a sting in the tail to these mar-

In some husky rats, the intermingling of white within colored hairs becomes excessively pronounced

kings. Young huskies have hardly any white hairs in their coats. Consequently, there is still a clear contrast at a young age between the white on their bellies and the color on their backs. Yet, as huskies grow older, starting from approximately eight weeks old, the number of white hairs intermingling among the colored ones steadily increases. As a rule, they become slightly lighter after each molt. In some huskies, this intermingling becomes excessively pronounced and can even turn them completely white by the age of three or four months.

Siamese and Russian rats

A Siamese rat bears a close resemblance to the Siamese cat. The Siamese is a pale sepia-brown color, but its body extremities (the muzzle, ears, tail, and back), referred to as "points," have a much stronger and darker coloration. The points may be blue or brown. Unlike the Siamese rat, the Russian is not sepia-brown but pale ivory with colored points.

The effect of temperature

Siamese and Russian rats have darker pigmentation on their extremities, such as the nose, ears, and tail, but how dark the extremities are depends on the air temperature. The warmer the air temperature, the more these darker areas tend to fade. Consequently, there will be less contrast between an animal's extremities and the rest of its body during the heat of summer than during the colder months of winter, when the darker parts of the body, so much a feature of these breeds, will be much more evident.

Pearl
The pearl rat's coat is pale silver-gray and cream with dark gray tips to each hair. This gives the rat a special sheen. The eyes are black. There is also a cinnamon pearl rat: a pale orange-brown animal with black eyes and hairs that are banded in three colors (cream, blue, and orange), as well as silver guard hairs and hair tips that create a shimmering effect.

Silvered
Silvered rats have some partly silver-colored hairs. The ideal is for them to have between a quarter and half of their hairs silver-colored, giving the coat a sparkling effect.

Odd-eyed rat

Included under this type are silver black and silver fawn rats.

Odd-eyed
The color of rats' eyes depends on their coat color. Some rats have differently colored eyes: either one pink and one dark ruby or else one pink and the other black. Odd-eyed specimens can occur in all kinds of color varieties.

Coat varieties
Rex
Rex rats have wavy or curly coats. Different hereditary factors are involved in producing the different types of rex coat, and the curliness of the coat depends on how much of the genetic factor for curliness is present. Some hereditary factors not only make the coat hair curl, but also the whiskers and even the eyelashes. The latter can cause particular health problems. A rex coat is not always perfectly even; sometimes bald or balding patches appear on the body.

Hairless
The hairless rat, also referred to as the sphinx rat, looks somewhat like an alien being due to its bald and wrinkly appearance. This variety has even been described as looking like a shaved miniature kangaroo. It is precisely this extraordinary look that so attracts some people. Some hairless rats are completely bald; others have a few tufts of

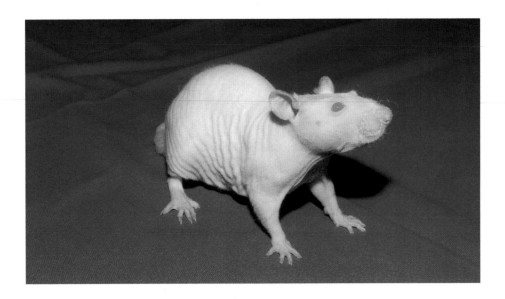

Hairless rat

The Dumbo rat has extra-large, drooping ears

downy hair left here and there, referred to as "fuzz" or "patchwork." Sometimes these rats are not truly hairless but the product of sustained crossings between rex rats. Depending on the coloration and markings that they ought to have, hairless rats may have pink or black skins and red or dark eyes. Because they lack a coat, hairless rats need special care. They have difficulty in keeping properly warm and rely on the presence of hirsute companions or

other sources of heat in order to regulate their body temperature. They often eat more in order to keep their body temperature up and thus need high-quality food. Their exposed skin is vulnerable to wounds from scratching and requires soft bedding material. Some hairless rats have weaker immune systems, making them more susceptible to diseases and allergic reactions. In practice, they appear not to live as long as rats with fur. Moreover, hairless females may have difficulty in suckling their young because they produce too little milk. This problem can be avoided by not using hairless females for breeding. There are females that carry the hairlessness gene, but nevertheless have fur. These can be mated with hairless males to produce hairless offspring.

Physical varieties
Dumbo rats
Dumbo rats have extra-large, low-set ears. The first Dumbo rats surfaced in the United States in the 1990s. They quickly became firm favorites as a result of their cartoon-like appearance. The shape of these large, rounded, "Dumbo the elephant" ears can vary. Some ears take the shape of rose petals; other ears are more rounded like the letter "C." A Dumbo rat's head is characteristically wider and flatter compared with the heads of rats with normal ears. According to some people, Dumbo rats are notable

Tailless rat

for having gentler, calmer, and quieter personalities—but some disagree. Perhaps it is merely the position of the ears that makes these animals look more "relaxed."

Tailless

The tailless rat is sometimes also called a Manx, after the tailless breed of cat of the same name. These animals have either no tail or only a short stump of a tail. In the absence of a tail, a rat's center of gravity shifts, causing it to develop a slightly different, more pear-shaped body frame compared with normal rats. The position of the hind legs is also different; the hindquarters look somewhat like those of a guinea pig. Breeding between tailless rats is advised against as it can produce rats with spinal column abnormalities. Moreover, female tailless rats may encounter problems in giving birth due to skeletal deformities, particularly the pelvis. Tailless rats can find it more difficult to regulate their body heat because they lack the thermoregulation provided by the tail. For that reason, it is additionally important to make sure that these animals do not overheat. Their supporters say that despite lacking a tail that grips and acts like a rudder, tailless rats can manage perfectly well and are just as nimble as animals with tails.

The rex factor can cause bald patches

Opponents contend that in a number of cases tailless rats are unable to move forward except by hopping and cannot sit up on their haunches, and they point out that malformed hindquarters can result in incontinence.

Being unusual does not always mean better

Many people think it is interesting to keep a pet that is unusual or different. After all, rats with unusually large ears, curly coats, or naked skin certainly get noticed. Others question the validity of these varieties. Isn't a rex rat with curled whiskers being deprived of its sense of touch? And are you really adding to the quality of an animal's life by removing its protective coat, or by depriving it of its tail's essential functions? With this in mind, some rat clubs have now decided to exclude hairless and tailless rats from their shows.

The future

Nowadays, rats are being bred with coats that are longer and softer, short and velvety, or extra glossy (satin). Dwarf varieties, half the size of normal fancy rats, are also appearing. Doubtless, the future will bring even more new colors, coats, and markings.

*Animals with
aberrant
coloration
sometimes have
poorer chances of
survival*

10 GLOSSARY

A litter: (or B, C, to Z litter) many rat fanciers give rats from one litter names beginning with the same letter, sometimes running through the alphabet starting with A.

Agouti: wild-type coloration

Barbering: nibbling at and excessive grooming of a rat's own coat or that of another rat; may be caused by stress

Berkshire: marked variety in which the rat has a white underside (belly)

Blaze: a white wedge-shaped mark on the forehead from the muzzle to the ears

Breed standard: The requirements of type, build, color, etc. that an animal must fulfill to qualify as a particular breed. Breed standards are set by national rat clubs, and may differ from country to country.

Bruxing: repetitive grinding of the incisors against each other; either an expression of contentment or stress

Buck: a male rat

Capped: rat with a colored marking on its head like a cap, not extending to the throat or past the ears

Doe: a female rat

Downunder: colored markings on a rat's belly, not only described as such because of their position but also because this variety originates from Australia

Dumbo: rat variety with extra-large, low-set ears

Ear-wiggle: females in estrus (entering their period of fertility) rapidly vibrate their ears as a message to males

Eel stripe: a colored stripe along the spine

Eye-boggle: the slight vibration of the eyeballs in and out of the sockets; seen in combination with teeth grinding (bruxing), caused by part of the rat's chewing muscle, which runs behind the eyeball

Fuzz: remnants or tufts of downy undercoat hairs sometimes appearing in hairless rats

Guard hairs: longer, coarser hairs that form an animal's outer coat and protect its undercoat

Head-bobbing: movement of the head up and down or side-to-side that gives the rat a better, sharper picture of its environment

Hooded: a marked variety in which the rat has a colored head and shoulders from which a stripe of color runs along its spine to its tail

Husky: rat with markings similar to those in husky dogs: inter-

mingled colored and white hairs on its back with a white belly and feet and blaze

Irish: colored rat marked with a white triangle on its chest between the forelegs

Kitten: commonly used name for young, pre-weaned rats

Litter: 1. the babies produced at one birth; 2. the animals' absorbent bedding material

Manx: name for a tailless rat

Masked: a white rat with a colored "mask" only across the face and around the eyes

Megacolon: an intestinal disorder that occurs principally in young rats making the transition from mother's milk to solid food

Mismarked: a disrespectful term to indicate that the color or markings do not comply fully with the standard (e.g. mismarked hooded rat)

Odd-eyed: a rat that has one pink eye and one eye dark ruby or black

Pedigree: document that records a rat's ancestry and any other data

Piloerection: describes a rat's hair standing on end; occurs when a rat is cold, stressed, or during or after an altercation (when it wants to appear larger and more imposing). Also referred to as "poofing"

Pinkie rat: a newborn rat that is still hairless with pink skin

Points: dark-tinted bodily extremities, such as the feet and muzzle, in the Siamese rat

Poofing: see Piloerection

Porphyrin: reddish-brown secretion produced by a gland behind the eyeball, seen around the nose and eyes, often erroneously assumed to be blood. The presence of porphyrin may indicate illness or stress

Pup: name used in the scientific community for young, pre-weaned rats

Rat king: a rare phenomenon in which several rats are discovered with their tails knotted together

Rattery: a place where rats are bred or where rat fanciers keep rats

Rattling: a wheezing, faltering breathing pattern; indicates that there is something wrong with the respiratory system

Rex: a rat variety with curly hair and curled whiskers

Silvered: colored rat with a coat that is evenly interspersed with white hairs

Sphinx: alternative name for hairless rats

Standard: description of how an ideal rat of its type should look in terms of external appearance

Swaying: see Head-bobbing
Ticking: banded colors on a hair with dark-tinted tips

11 RATS ON THE INTERNET

Typing the word "rat" into an Internet search engine is a cast-iron guarantee of hours of surfing fun. The websites given below are good places to start.

Clubs especially for rat enthusiasts in the United States and Canada:
Rat and Mouse Club of America (RMCA)
13075 Springdale Street, PMB 302,
Westminster CA 92683
www.rmca.org
American Fancy Rat and Mouse Association (AFRMA)
AFRMA Secretary, 9230 64th Street,
Riverside CA 92509-5924
www.afrma.org
Rat Fan Club
857 Lindo Lane,
Chico CA 95973
www.ratfanclub.org
Pet Rats Canada
www.petratscanada.com

Informative English-language websites about rats:
The Ratster: breeder and information directory
www.ratster.com
Anne's Rat Page
www.ratbehavior.org
The Laboratory Rat: A Natural History
www.ratlife.org
Rat Guide (Health, Medication, and Care of Pet Rats)
http://ratguide.com
Petrat
http://petrat.ca

The author's website — with link page (Dutch-language)
Rattery van de Waterratten
www.judithlissenberg.homestead.com

Acrobatics on
a rope ladder

Credits and photography

The author is indebted to all the pet rat owners who were kind enough to provide her with useful information and/or to allow their animals to be photographed. Special thanks are due to Jiska Sanders-van Soest of the Nieuw Hamelen Rattery for her invaluable advice and to Esther Verhoef of FurryTails with whom it has been such a pleasure to work.

The author has carefully scrutinized all of the advice and information in this book, which, as far as possible, has been supported and verified through the study of source material and according to the most recently available data. This notwithstanding, neither the author nor the publisher can be held liable for any consequences that may arise from the advice given.

All of the photographs in this publication were taken by Judith Lissenberg.